All Scripture references taken from the KJV of the Holy Bible, unless otherwise indicated.

WHEN THE TABLE IS SET AGAINST YOU

by Dr. Marlene Miles

Freshwater Press 2026

Freshwaterpress9@gmail.com

ISBN: 978-1-971933-13-9

Paperback Version

Copyright 2026, Dr. Marlene Miles

All rights reserved. No part of this book may be reproduced, distributed, or transmitted by any means or in any means including photocopying, recording or other electronic or mechanical methods without prior written permission of the publisher except in the case of brief publications or critical reviews.

Table of Contents

WHEN THE TABLE IS SET AGAINST YOU

Freshwater

Psalm 23

The Lord is my shepherd; I shall not want.

He maketh me to lie down in green pastures: he leadeth me beside the still waters.

He restoreth my soul: he leadeth me in the paths of righteousness for his name's sake.

Yea, though I walk through the valley of the shadow of death, I will fear no evil: for thou art with me; thy rod and thy staff they comfort me.

Thou preparest a table before me in the presence of mine enemies: thou anointest my head with oil; my cup runneth over.

Surely goodness and mercy shall follow me all the days of my life: and I will dwell in the house of the Lord for ever.

IN THE PRESENCE OF MY ENEMIES

You prepare a table before me **in the presence of my enemies. (v. 5)**

Psalm 23 does not say the enemies are removed; they are there, and the table is set anyway. That one phrase forces us to ask what *presence* means. The Hebrew implication of the meaning of *presence* is nearness without permission. The enemies are: Close enough to see what's going on, and see what you are doing. They are close enough to smell the bread, Close enough to hear the blessing that is snot prepared for them. They are not authorized to partake of the meal, the blessing, or anything God has prepared for you. but still they hover.

This is not absence of threat. It is containment of threat. As long as GOD is there, you don't care that the enemies are near, *do you?*

The table that the LORD has prepared is declarative: This is the Lord's table, the enemies know to get back, stay back, and they do not try to attack because the Good Shepherd is there.

Three possible positions of the enemy at the table. They can be as observers or watchers. They are nearby, standing, monitoring. They see the oil poured. They watch the cup run over. They cannot interrupt the host; because the Host is the Lord.

This is restraint, not reconciliation. They are not **invited** in the sense that we are.

Another position could be that they are resentful onlookers, drooling ones. They want the benefits without the covenant. They may not want the food, but they want the blessings. They covet the seat that we sit in. They may not want to be nearby, but they'd like to snatch that authority and go and use it their way—which we know will be evil if they use it. They resent the favor, the favor God shows His own—mankind. They despise the host's choice: US.

This is where jealousy hardens into bitterness.

Lord, I rebuke the spirit of jealousy, envy, unforgiveness, covetous, resentment and bitterness and the ones who carrying it and will not let it go, in the Name of Jesus. Lord, clear my life and table of these disruptions and distractions, in the Name of Jesus. Amen.

The third and the best example of the Enemy *at* the table is Judas. He was **AT** the Lord's table--, not just his presence, but his person was there– right beside Jesus. This is the most dangerous position. The psalm does not specify distance, only *presence*. Judas was **there**. Scripture later shows us a table where bread was shared and words were spoken. This would not have been possible, except the Lord agreed to it prior to its occurrence.

Judas Iscariot sits in the seat of betrayal.

Before the betrayal by Judas, Jesus did something that looks unrelated regarding the table. It looks like it is not related, but it is. In the Gospels, Jesus overturns the tables of the moneychangers. This was not a random act of anger or rage. It was prophetic. Jesus announced by this act, *"This table system is harsh and unfair and distracting in the house of God." It is a whole competing altar, so He overturns it.*

But Jesus is doing something else here: He is stating that no table where wickedness is allowed or where evil sneaks in, or is allowed is going to prosper will decide **My value**. Even all the money on the money changer's table is not enough to match the value of the Lord.

Later, Jesus will sit at a table with the very one who negotiated a price for Him, valued Him at thirty pieces of silver and sold Him for that price, which was the price of a slave. That transaction is recorded in the Gospel of Matthew. The same system He overturned will try to re-price Him, re-name Him, re-brand Him and call Him a slave.

Lord, let no evil, fake, false or counterfeit table that I am called to or have to sit at be able to buy me, to sell me, to use me, to steal from me, to take from me, rebrand me, stamp me, change my name or my value, in the Name of Jesus. AMEN.

I am not who *they* think I am. I am not who *they* say I am. I am in Christ. I belong to the Lord Jesus Christ. I AM who HE says I am and my value is precious, in the Name of Jesus.. I will not be devalued or discounted at any table, in the Name of Jesus. AMEN

There is a table in the Upper Room, **but** Jesus does **not** overturn *that* table. He sits. He breaks bread. He allows the enemy proximity.

Why?

He did it for us

That table was about **authority**. The betrayal at that table, however, does not cancel the covenant. The cost that mere men, evil men agreed upon doesn't change Jesus' value, His Name or His authority. The sale does not nullify the Sonship; it does not change the relationship with the Father, who is in Heaven. The enemy's presence **<u>NEVER</u>** stops the Father's preparation.

Sometimes the LORD wants the enemy there, close by for His own purposes. (more on this in my book **<u>Seasons of Siege: God is Coming</u>** – link in the credits)

The enemy's presence, the enemy's plans and even their words and descriptions do not change who **<u>you</u>** are to God. It does not change your value in Christ, your worth in the Kingdom, or your destiny. As long as you remain steadfast in the Lord, they cannot change your relationship with the Father, who is in Heaven. Amen.

PSALM 23 REFRAMED

So, when the Psalmist says: *"You prepare a table before me in the presence of my enemies…"* It means: They may watch, but they won't rule; God is in charge. They may sit, but they won't own. They may betray, rename, cast aspersions, cast evil imaginations, or try to trick or initiate, but that won't define or redefine you. You are in Christ and you are HIS. Amen.

That they are near or *at* the table is not approval--, it is their exposure. The boldness, the nerve to show themselves as if they have rights or if they belong, or it they are strong. The nerve. God may not remove every enemy, but He will remove their authority over the table. *When the Table Has Been Set Against You*, God knows, and He will handle it.

Psalm 23 doesn't end at the *presence of the enemy*. It moves to action. *God prepares the table.*

Prepare means *arrange deliberately,* and just as deliberately, re-arrange if necessary. So, when a table has been set against you with rigged seating, false terms, predetermined outcomes, hidden agendas and hidden prices with secrets, trickery, deception and lies or maybe even defiled or poison food, God will handle that. When you are His own, His beloved, God will clear the table; He will overturn it.

God does not argue with the guests; if He didn't set the table, and He is not *allowing* the table, it is subject to destruction. If that table is defiled or corrupt, He will overturn, remove, or destroy it.

Table-wiping is a Biblical pattern of table reset. God's resets are not mild or gentle corrections; they are clean sweeps. Old agreements are invalidated. Hidden negotiations and treachery are exposed. Unspoken expectations are canceled. Ungodly plans are wiped out.

Nothing on the table survives the wipe, not the food, the coins, the money, the contracts, the papers, NOTHING--, not even the ungodly plans that they have ungodly planned against you when they set the table against you, stacked the odds against you and invited you to something that God is not involved in.

You are God's and therefore, there are some things that are NOT even allowed because of whose you are and your covenant with Him. You must know it and decree it. Some things are not allowed because of my covenant with God. The wicked ones at the table may say they are of God or from God, but we shall know them by their *fruit.* and that by discernment.

40 DAYS WITHOUT A TABLE

Jesus modeled this before living it. Jesus learned how to recognize every kind of table. First, He turned down 40 days and nights of **tables** after He had fasted 40 days.

Forty doesn't mean long , it means *long enough.* Forty marks the time required for God's purpose to mature. Biblically, forty is completion of process, not excess of time.

Before Jesus ever sat at tables with sinners, rulers, Pharisees, disciples, or betrayers, He learned how to refuse them. Jesus bypassed tables before overturned one. He overturned tables before He sat at one that became hostile, even while He was seated at it.

Jesus showed us: *"I recognize corrupt systems before I submit to prophetic necessity.*

Forty days without a table an education of authority for Him, possibly, or it was a lesson and demonstration for us. After His baptism, Jesus Christ is led into the wilderness for 40 days. That is not accidental timing. That is table training.

For forty days there were no communal meals. No social validation. No religious audience. No economic system. No "king's dainties." Only hunger, silence, and the Word. This is where Jesus learns, *I do not eat by invitation. I eat by authorization. This is a good lesson for folks who have their feet under just about anyone's table.*

After fasting in the Wilderness, the very first temptation is a table. The enemy doesn't start with power or worship. He starts with bread, saying, "If You are the Son of God, command these stones to become bread." In that temptation, it is not about food. That's about who decides when, what, and how Jesus eats, and how He uses power. The enemy wants to do the same to you. Jesus refuses to give in, so should you. So should we all.

Lord, anyone who wants to control or end my staff of bread, let them have what they want for me, for themselves, instead of me, in the Name of Jesus. Amen.

Jesus refuses. So must you. Not because bread is evil, but because **this table was not set by the Father**.

If the devil is inviting you to dinner, are you going to go? Especially if the Lord has called you to fast, will you instead take up the devil's offer to dine? Hold this truth: if you have been instructed to fast, the enemy will feed you. Whether we abound or are abased we learn to be satisfied. That is what Jesus was modeling for us.

In those 40 days, Jesus learned hunger does not define Him. Appetite does not govern Him; He governs appetite. Provision cannot be divorced from obedience. No table is neutral. *These questions can be asked: is the exchange at this table? Is it godly? Is it acceptable? Or is it evil and entrapment?*

By the time He leaves the wilderness, Jesus knows which tables to sit at, Which tables to confront, Which to overturn, which tables to allow betrayal at, and which tables to replace entirely. That discernment was forged before ministry, not during it.

This is why Jesus could overturn tables later on. When Jesus overturns tables in the temple, it is not on an impulse; it is educated authority… He had already lived 40 days without tables. So, when He saw that table in the Temple, He saw: Priced access to God. He saw: Unfair exchanges. He saw: a competing altar in the House of God. He saw: distracted worship. And so, He ends them without hesitation.

Because He already proved: *I can live without your bread. Without your table.*

AUTHORITY & GOVERNANCE

Authority precedes appetite because rank determines protocol. Scripture is consistent on this: those entrusted with authority are not only governed differently, they are expected to govern *themselves* well prior to receiving certain levels of authority. Well, in God's system. On the dark side, authority and wealth are often sought to circumvent God and His requirements.

Authority changes the rules of engagement In the Bible, status is not about privilege first — it's about restraint first. A king, priest, or steward of authority is never free to act "like everyone else," because their actions teach, authorize, and set precedent. That's why Scripture holds leaders to *stricter protocols*.

Biblical Pattern: Higher authority requires higher restraint. King David, for example, could not eat the same way Saul did, speak the same way, or act impulsively without consequence. When appetite governed him (Bathsheba), the fallout was familial, generational and even national not just private.

Melchizedek hosts a table of bread and wine with no leverage, no demand, no appetite-driven exchange. His restraint at that table *confirms* his authority, and Abraham's participation confirmed his own identity. Together, this exchange confirms rightful order.

Jesus Christ, as the Highest Authority, His restraint is the most severe. He refuses bread in hunger. He refuses spectacle in temptation. He refuses power without obedience. He refuses to call Angels to defend Himself. Authority governs appetite, not the other way around. Appetite has been known to destroy authority; so we must be very careful.

When dining with a rich man be on your guard and don't stuff yourself, though it all tastes so good; for he is trying to bribe you, and no good is going to come of his invitation. (Proverbs 23:2-3)

Lower or low estate people live by different rules. Those of low estate often live by urgency. They eat when they can. Take what's offered, survive first, discern later. Scripture *acknowledges* this reality without celebrating it. People in survival mode are most concerned with staying alive, and that foremost includes what shall they eat, or do they even have food to eat?

But those entrusted with authority who must live by order will live differently than those who wield little to no authority. Those in authority can afford to wait, discern, govern desire, and refuse what compromises standing. That's not elitism; that's stewardship. A young lady once told me that her grandmother told her, "Its amazing that you are never hungry until you have no money." Look how that temptation works, whatever the flesh feels it doesn't have, that is not only what it wants, that is also what will be brought in as a temptation. Even if the temptation is not in the natural, but only in the mind. When the man of low estate, even if it is only temporary is aware of his lack or poverty, that is when he is hungry. Said another way, that is when appetite announces itself and that man may then begin to seek all the wrong things. Appetite is the magnet that draws men to many kinds of tables, not just dinner tables.

Kings are judged more harshly because their appetite affects others. Their choices authorize behavior, and their tables train nations. Protocols *are* different for people of different orders or classes. Pay close attention here: Scripture recognizes three realities at once. A man can be born into low estate sby oppression, injustice, lack of opportunity, famine, exile. A man's appetite can keep him there. A man's appetite can also *lower* him further. Ungoverned appetite prevents transition.

Those of low estate may live by urgency; those of authority must live by order. Appetite may be excusable in survival — but never in stewardship.

DIFFERENT TABLES

In Psalm 23, God prepares the table. In Proverbs 23 we are warned of a table that God did not prepare and we are told, *Don't desire deceptive dainties*. In the Book of Job, we see where tables become distraction. Jezebel's table is one of evil initiation, evil alliances and patronage.

In the Upper Room we see a table the Lord had prepared, but it turned hostile. In the Wilderness, Jesus refused the hostile table or evil opportunity. Jesus modeled what happens when evil tables are refused.

Jesus learned authority over tables by living without them. **You cannot govern tables that are already governing you**. The only way a table can govern you is if it owns you. More specifically, if it owns your authority. That means that you exchanged or gave your authority away, had it solen, or traded with it, your governance is gone. That could also mean that you were **sold** at that table.

So, make sure you don't let anyone sell you.

AND make sure you don't sell yourself not for a buck, a piece of bread, prestige, promotion, pride, or promised prosperity.

Fasting is to prove that what you are fasting, or what you are fasting about doesn't own you. One year I fasted chocolate the whole year – I had to--, chocolate cravings were trying to take over. I've fasted a lot of things at different times. For example: For years, I listened to no music and watched no TV – I wasn't trying to prove a point; I just wasn't interested. I also refused to just do what everyone else was doing just to fit in. Suppose that made me one of the uncool kids--- oh well. Today, I can take or leave chocolate, TV, and all kinds of worldly stuff. That means I can govern it, because it is not governing me.

This is how you rise in authority.

So, when the thing you are supposed to have authority over has already overtaken you – what do you do? God gave Adam and eve authority over everything that god had created—instead of exercising authority over that apple – they ate it. They gave their authority away—traded it for food. They traded it for an apple, or whatever else they got; many say it was not an apple. Whatever it was, Jesus had to come and buy us back. They could have traded that authority for the knowledge of good and evil, which the apple was the *fruit* of that tree.

Jesus didn't give in to temptations, so later, when He sits at the table of betrayal, He is not trapped; He is **sovereign over it**. When you are facing the thing that you have worshipped, then it is your master. At that time, you cannot be master over it.

COMMON TABLES

Tables we commonly sit at, whether we realize it or not, will be listed in a very organized way in this chapter.

Where does danger most often hide in plain sight? The following are lists of common table "types" ranked by most likely to be *bait*. These are tables that look normal, benevolent, or even Godly, but are frequently used as disguises for governance transfer. I'll go from lowest apparent risk to highest risk, because deception almost always works in that direction.

Lowest apparent risk is the table that is usually honest and overt in purpose. These tables are rarely disguised because their function is explicit. Risk exists, but deception is low.

Judicial & Conflict

- Trial table
- Plea table

- Judgment table
- Accusation table
- Defense table

This first table list is low disguise risk because they are what they are. Everyone knows these tables are adversarial. You come guarded. You expect consequences. No one pretends these are about comfort. These tables may be severe, but they are not subtle.

Next, showing a more moderate risk; the power is clear and the terms are usually well explained

Institutional & Public

- Boardroom table
- Conference table
- Strategy table
- Policy table
- Leadership table
- Advisory table
- Roundtable discussion

Risk profile: Power dynamics are real but generally named. Danger enters when the flattery and false talk start. Gentle, but informal influence and "off-the-record" conversations signal the start of more danger. Still, these tables usually announce authority, so discernment is easier.

Moderate to high risk tables are transactional, but they are masked as being fair, when they are not.

Transactional & Power-Based

- Bargaining table

- Negotiation table

- Settlement table

- Contract table

- Deal-making table

- Arbitration table

- Mediation table

These tables *claim* neutrality but often favor the party with leverage. Treachery may be commonly disguised behind words like, "Fairness," "mutual benefit," "compromise. The hidden danger is that a person can lose authority legally and willingly, while believing they are being reasonable.

High Risk tables appear where necessity has created vulnerabilities. The enemy is adept at creating problems and then jumping in to pretend to help you solve them.

Economic & Survival

- Employment table
- Payroll table
- Benefits table
- Aid table
- Sponsorship table
- Patronage table

Risk increases at these tables because survival pressure lowers discernment thresholds. Most dangerous among those in this category are the Patronage table and the Sponsorship table. These often require unspoken allegiance. When survival is involved, people confuse provision with permission. These tables are often weaponized against authority.

Very High Risk tables look safe, they feel normal, but they are often bait.

Relational & Personal

- Dinner table
- Dating table
- Family table
- Holiday table
- Reconciliation table
- Estrangement table

- Counseling table

- Friendship table

This is the most common bait category because it looks harmless, loving, relational, even holy. The #1 disguised table in all of Scripture and life is the Dinner Table.

Why?

Because food disarms. Familiarity lowers guard. Proximity creates obligation. Courtesy suppresses discernment. The Dating table is a close second, in this category, especially when one party is hosting, provision is unequal, intent is unclear.

Many people lose authority at tables they never thought to evaluate.

very high risk (spiritually weighted — must be discerned).

Spiritual & Moral

- Teaching table
- Discipleship table
- Confession table
- Repentance table
- Altar table
- Communion table

These are high risk not because they are bad, but because they are powerful. These are dangerous when corrupted because spiritual authority amplifies impact. Trust is assumed. Resistance is framed as rebellion.

False spiritual tables do the absolute most damage, because they claim divine legitimacy.

The next category represents Extreme Risks. These tables are openly corrupt and are insidious—they are not often entered quickly, suddenly or all at once. They are most often entered into gradually by smooth invitations or seduction.

Counterfeit / Corrupt

- Jezebel's table
- King's dainties table
- Moneychangers' table
- Bribery table
- Compromise table
- Silence-for-provision table
- Pay-to-play table

These tables are rarely entered *directly*. They are almost always reached through another table first. Most common gateway tables to the extreme risk tables:

- Dinner table

- Aid table
- Patronage table
- Teaching table

Highest risk of all (the true entry point) is often the most overlooked are the Internal Tables.

Internal

- Decision-making table
- Imagination table
- Memory table
- Appetite table
- Fear table
- Desire table

This is where all other tables gain access. If these are ungoverned, then no external table is safe. No host needs power. No manipulation is required. Every hostile table succeeds only after an internal table is compromised.

Of all these categories, the most dangerous disguise table overall is still the Dinner table. Because it looks like nothing. It is so common, people eat every day; most several times a day. Your first experiences with the dinner table was with your parents and family, so it *seems* normal, safe.

The most dangerous gateway tables are Dating tables, Aid / Patronage table, and Teaching table.

Most decisive table are the internal tables, especially appetite and fear. The most dangerous tables are not the ones marked as corrupt, but the ones we never think to discern. No table can govern you unless one inside you agree to it.

Greater is he that is in us than he that is in the world.

We move through life from table to table, but few of us pause long enough to ask which ones are shaping us — and which ones we should leave. Not every table feeds the body; some quietly govern the soul.

A casino table is **not neutral**, and it doesn't belong in just one category. It's a **hybrid table**, which is what makes it especially dangerous. Primarily it is a c**ounterfeit / Corrupt Table.** A casino table is fundamentally a **counterfeit provision table** that promises gain without stewardship, reward without labor, advancement without authority, and relief without formation. That places it in *false tables*.

Secondarily it is an **Appetite Table. It causes the body to generate** dopamine, urgency, "one more", emotional hunger disguised as chance, directly testing **ungoverned hunger** It is also a transaction table. You pay to play, pay to sit, the house sets the terms. It *looks* voluntary but is structurally exploitative.

A casino table gives the feeling of control choices, timing, strategy, rituals, but no actual authority. The house governs everything from the odds to the duration, reward thresholds, and losses. This This is simulated authority — and simulated authority is a trap. A casino table answers appetite immediately and self governance and authority, never. This is why people stay seated. It is the textbook example of Provision without authority. A casino table is where appetite is rewarded just enough to keep authority from ever transferring.

Some of us may have a favorite snack chip. You take a bite and it's got that flavor you like, but not *quite* enough of it, so you eat another and then another trying to reach that flavor satisfaction. The full authority of that flavor is not in the bag. Trust me.

The casino table doesn't just take the gambler's money, it trains that gambler to sit, and sit, and be owned. Owned by the house. It is addictive and that is it's featured purpose. Other tables are addictive as a by product. Other potentially addictive tables are: 1. Approval validation tables. 2. Provision tables. 3. Power-adjacent tables, and 4. Conflict tables.

WHEN THE TABLE TURNS HOSTILE

A table does not usually announce its hostility. Most turn gradually, not suddenly. That's why discernment is not about paranoia, it's about pattern recognition. How do you know when a table has turned hostile when authority dynamics shift against you, even if the tone remains polite.

Common Indicators can include, but this is not an exhaustive list.

1. Terms change without discussion What was once optional becomes assumed. What was once mutual becomes expected.

2. Silence is interpreted as agreement. Your lack of objection is used as endorsement.

3. Boundaries are tested, then pressured. Not attacked outright — *normalized*.

4. Provision becomes leverage. Past generosity is referenced to justify present control.

5. You feel pressure to stay seated. Discomfort increases, but leaving feels "impolite," "dramatic," or "disloyal."

6. You begin explaining yourself excessively. Authority erosion often shows up as over-justification.

When two or more of these are present, the table is no longer neutral.

HOW TO CONDUCT YOURSELF AT A HOSTILE TABLE

The goal is not confrontation when you have found yourself at a hostile table. The goal is preservation of authority. You do not need to expose hostility to respond to it. If you get up and leave, you do not owe explanations for withdrawal. You do not correct hosts who benefit from misunderstanding. You do not negotiate at tables designed to extract from you. Often, the most authoritative move is shortened presence.

There are times when you know or suspect the table will turn hostile on you when you should not go alone. There are tables where solo presence increases risk. Never Go Alone when the power imbalance is severe. Don't go alone when survival, livelihood, or reputation is involved. Go with witness or counsel when Legal, financial, or institutional authority is present. Don't go alone if you are emotionally vulnerable. And don't go alone if the table has a history of coercion or misrepresentation.

In these cases, know that witnesses protect authority. Presence becomes documentation. Silence becomes dangerous. Going alone here is not courage it's exposure.

Still, there are times when you must go all alone. There are also tables where going alone is required. You must go alone when The issue is internal alignment. The decision concerns withdrawal or refusal. Authority must be reclaimed personally. Influence would dilute clarity. You are exiting rather than negotiating

At these tables, companions can blur responsibility. Consensus is not needed or can weaken resolve. Authority must be exercised without validation. Some tables require solitude because authority cannot be delegated.

Presence with others is for protection. Presence alone is for alignment. Knowing the difference is Wisdom. At a hostile Table, don't explain your discernment. Don't argue intent. Don't rehearse history. Don't appeal to fairness. Don't wait for permission to leave.

Hostile tables do not respond to clarity — they respond to loss of access. A table becomes hostile when your authority begins to cost you comfort. You don't need proof a table is hostile; you need discernment that it no longer serves covenant.

Knowing when to leave is not weakness — it is governance."

A table turns hostile when it requires from you what God does not require, or disregards what God does require. A table becomes hostile when God is ignored, minimized, or displaced. When obedience to God is subtly penalized. When additional requirements are imposed beyond Scripture. When fear, pressure, or obligation replaces freedom. When human authority begins to rival divine authority. This includes legalism, coercion, spiritual intimidation, transactional "obedience, implied penalties for non-compliance. At that point, the issue is no longer fellowship it is governance.

God's covenant is sufficient. Anything added to it is not "extra holiness" — it is competition. Scripture is clear; God governs by truth and freedom. Counterfeit authority governs by pressure and demand

So, when a table begins to demand loyalty God did not request, require silence God did not command, exact payment God did not authorize, then that table has crossed from neutral to hostile.

The table turned hostile when it began asking of me what God never asked. When a table requires what God does not, it has already overstepped.

Discernment shows you the table; wisdom tells you when it has turned.

YOU CANNOT SERVE TWO MASTERS

What Jesus is really saying in the Gospel of Matthew 6:24 (also echoed in Gospel of Luke 16:13): *"No one can serve two masters…"*

Jesus does not say that y*ou might have a master, or that some people choose to serve.* He says, "No one can serve two." The implication is unavoidable: Man will serve a master. The only variable is which one.

The implication here is that the master that man serves will be spirit and what manifests in the natural after that spiritual choice is made will clarify even more who or what man chose to worship.

Mastery Is Assumed, Not Optional. Jesus frames mastery as a given, not a moral failure.

Why?

Because to live as a human is to obey something; we were built to worship. It means that man will organize life around something. He will take direction from something, ad he will give loyalty to something.

That "something" functions as a master, whether named or not.

So the real choice is not *freedom vs submission*. Instead, it is Who (Or what) governs you?

Do people who claim "i have no master" live in deception? Biblically speaking — yes, but not always consciously. Those who claim to have no master are usually governed by something. Agnostics and atheists, those who believe in nothing are governed by something – it is unavoidable, not just because of how we are made, but because we are not solitary, individual islands. So these things may have mastery over a man: appetite, fear, approval, money, autonomy itself, self-preservation, desire for control, self.

Scripture never treats autonomy as neutral. In fact, Paul later describes this condition plainly, people become "slaves" to what they obey (Romans 6). So, the deception is this: Mistaking unconscious submission for freedom.

Jesus Names Money (Mammon)—it is the only idol in the Bible called a master. Jesus doesn't randomly pick money as the rival master. Money promises security, demands loyalty, rewards trust, punishes dependence on God, shapes decisions.

That's why Jesus says you will love one, hate the other, cling to one, despise the other. Those are

relational words, not abstract or transactional words. Masters don't just command — they **form affection.**

Every table answers the master question. Who sets it? Who supplies it? Who defines the terms? Who expects loyalty afterward?

This is why Jezebel's table required obedience. Judas' table divided allegiance. Esau's appetite ruled inheritance, Jesus' wilderness fast broke mastery. Communion restores right allegiance. You cannot serve two masters. because tables always train allegiance.

Jesus assumes every person will serve a master. The deception is not in serving — it is in believing we are free because we refuse to name the one we obey. Those who claim to have no master are usually governed by the one they least want to examine.

This is not condemnation; it's diagnosis. Jesus exposes mastery so people can choose rightly, not so they can be shamed.

You cannot govern tables that are already governing you. Mammon is one of those "tables." Mammon was not imposed on man; man installed it. Jesus speaks of Mammon as a master because man elevated it into that role. Money didn't seize authority. It was granted authority by human obedience. People actually live like this: If the money says yes then the answer is yes. If the money says no, then the answer is no. If the credit card goes through, then permission is granted. But, if the credit card declines, then the desire is denied. Fingers crossed, wishing and hoping. Praying to GOD that Mammon says it's okay for you to get a new car?

That is functional lordship; it is idolatry. Mammon doesn't need a voice. It rules by permission structures. That's why Jesus treats it as a rival master — not an object.

From cattle indicating wealth, exchange, and sustenance, man evolved into other types of currency. Cattle were alive, they reproduced, they were messy and they required stewardship. They tied wealth to creation and care. They are a lot of work. Cattle could not be abstracted from responsibility.

They were also used in worship, which mattered: Wealth was acknowledged as belonging to God. Sacrifice reminded man he was not autonomous

The prophetic shift was when man went from living wealth to dead wealth. When man moved from livestock to metal as currency, something profound happened. Metal is "dead" in that it does not reproduce, does not require care, does not age biologically, because it is not alive. The image on it, if it is a coin, can become dated, but it doesn't age, for example. Metal does not die, does not cry out and it does not remind you of dependence. This is how it can become or be made into an idol.

It can be hoarded, hidden, stored, controlled. This was not just economic innovation. It was a shift in trust.

Silver was skipped because gold Is Incorruptible. Gold doesn't rust, but silver can tarnish. Prophetically, this mimics divine attributes of permanence, endurance, and reliability. Also in terms of value, gold is considered far more valuable than silver. Silver reminds you something needs maintenance. Gold lets you forget.

Gold centralizes power faster. Silver historically functioned as daily exchange, local trade, and transactional currency. Silver was in your basket. Gold was in your store. Gold functioned as stored power, imperial wealth, and kingly reserve. It was for war funding, national confidence.

Gold is not about buying bread. It's about commanding systems. Man skipped silver because silver keeps wealth *circulating*. Gold backs the seen wealth and allows wealth to concentrate. Gold replaces dependence with control. Cattle required God's blessing. Rain, land, grass, health, protection. Gold requires vaults and force, but it tries to move God out of the equation. Once wealth becomes gold, trust shifts from God to self and then to security systems. Provision shifts from blessing to possession dependence shifts from heaven to holdings.

That's not neutral. And that's one of the reasons why Jesus turned the money changing table over in the Temple. Also, look at the ark of the covenant, for example, Gold is used in sacred contexts. The Bible repeatedly warns against trusting it

Gold is not evil, but it is dangerously convincing. It *looks* eternal. It *feels* secure. It *pretends* to save.

That's why Mammon works.

Mammon doesn't ask, "Is this right?" Instead it asks, "Can you afford it?" And when *that* becomes the deciding factor, money has become master.

That's exactly what Jesus names.

Man did not discover Mammon, but he did enthrone it. Gold did not replace cattle because it was better; it replaced it because it required no faith.

WHAT IS THIS HERE?

So, you're at the table. Discern the table. Who else is at that table? Oh, but first who are you before you ever sat down at that table? Who are you?

The order of discernment. before any decision about staying, leaving, or overturning a table can be made, discernment must proceed in order.

Discern the table. Not every table is covenantal. Some are transactional. Some are disciplinary. Some are distractions. Some are traps. The first question is never *"What's being served?"* What kind of table is this?

Know who set the table. Tables carry the nature of their host. Who prepared it? Who sustains it? Who controls access? Who benefits if you remain seated? Is God at the table, or His representative? Perhaps you should get up right then. In discerning the table.... who's at the table? Is God at the table, or His representative? If not, then maybe you should get up and leave right then. the only other choices there then will be the flesh of man and darkness. The table is not neutral; it is hosted by God or *not*-God.

If God is not at the table, and His authority is not represented, then the only forces left to govern it are the flesh of man and entities from the kingdom of darkness. At that point, discernment is no longer complicated. You do not negotiate at tables God does not host. As a matter of fact, and as a matter of who you are in Christ, once you know who you are and walk in our rightful authority, you will know that God is the only one who can call you to a meeting. Can your subordinates call you to a board meeting at work? Can you call your boss to a meeting? Of course not.

If God is not there and not represented, slide your chair back, stand up and leave. By doing so, you preserve authority. Scripture does not present tables as morally undecided spaces. They are covenantal, transactional, or sacrificial by nature. A table will be governed by God's presence and order, or Human appetite and power, or dark spiritual influence. There is no fourth option. When God is absent, neutrality is a myth. Something else is already presiding.

Who is authorized to set the terms here? Then test it: Is truth honored, even when inconvenient? Is obedience to God protected—or penalized? Is silence rewarded? Is pressure subtle but persistent? Is compliance assumed simply because you showed up?

If God's authority is not welcome, your authority will be eroded. If God is not welcome at the table, neither am I. Leaving a table like this is alignment and it is Wisdom. Refuse to be governed by what God did not authorize.

Discern the purpose of the table. Some tables are for nourishment, instruction, restoration, judgment, exposure, or transition. A table meant for one purpose becomes dangerous when used for another. You must know why you are there. Discern who else is there, and how proximity matters. *Who is seated? Who is standing? Who is observing? Who is serving? Who is allowed to come and go freely?* And most importantly, *Who has influence at this table — formally or informally?*

Foremost, know Who *you* are at the table. This is the question beyond all the others, are you a guest? a servant? a son or daughter? a covenant partner? a negotiator? a witness? a sacrifice?

The table will treat you according to the role you accept, not the one you hope it assigns. If you don't know who you are in relation to the table, the table will define you, for you.

You can discern the table perfectly and still be undone if you have not discerned your authority in relation to it. Because tables don't just feed folks, they train identity. The most dangerous tables are not the ones we fail to discern, but the ones we enter without knowing who we are. No table is neutral to the one who sits unaware of their standing.

GAVE IT AWAY

What you worship does not steal your authority, you transfer it. Idols do not *take* governance by force. They receive it by consent. In Scripture, God consistently honors human agency. Authority is delegated, not seized.

When Jesus says, ***"You cannot serve two masters"*** (Matthew 6:24), He assumes that service is voluntary. Allegiance is chosen, and mastery is relational. Giving is worship and it is supposed to be done cheerfully, implying by choice, by one's own free will.

A master is not a thief; a master is obeyed. So, when something is worshiped, attention is redirected, trust is reassigned, obedience is yielded, decision-making is deferred. That is authority transfer, not hijacking.

Biblically and governance-wise, worship is not just singing or reverence. It is alignment of obedience. So, the sequence is: You yield trust. You yield obedience. Then after you yield decision authority, governance follows. That's why Paul can say people become *"slaves of the one they obey"* (Romans 6:16). Notice: *obey* comes before *slave*. Submission precedes mastery.

It feels like they "take over, but really authority is given, not taken or stolen. Once authority is transferred, the idol begins to set limits. It issues consequences. It demands maintenance. It reshapes priorities. You can hear or sense what they are demanding because they are enthroned in your life, so their voice is one that you hear and are expected to obey. At that point, it **feels** like usurpation, but biblically, it's the *fruit* of earlier consent.

That's why Scripture repeatedly says idols are *nothing* in themselves, powerless without worship. dependent on human allegiance. They rule only where they are enthroned. This proves the governing principle that you cannot govern what you worship, because worship is the act of transferring authority. Idols do not seize authority, but they set up conditions to receive it.

What governs you does so because you have entrusted it with decision-making power. Worship is not admiration — it is authorization.

Reset, which we will get to later in this book is possible because authority was given, not stolen. So, in the relinquishing of authority, what you worship governs you, not because it is powerful, but because you authorized it.

Let's say a passport grants you travel to go here or there and to do this or that. Mankind must look at all the places we can go with this human-alive-in-the-Earth passport. We use our passport wisely and correctly. It is not to patch holes in shoes or the roof of our houses. We do not burn it for warmth. It is our authority.

And yet man keeps using what grants access to try to solve what requires provision. Think of provision being for the body (flesh) and authority is for the spiritual things that concern a man. We must know the difference.

When a person uses a passport to patch a shoe, tile a roof, or burn for heat, they're not being creative. They're being desperate and misaligned. They are solving an *immediate need* by destroying a *long-term authority*. That is exactly what Scripture shows again and again. Esau burns his passport for stew. Judas trades his passport for silver--, not even gold, but just silver to be used up tomorrow. Adam spends his passport on fruit. Jezebel's prophets rent theirs for food, not because they lacked value but because they lacked discernment of what they were holding.

A man graduates from asking for provision when he realizes provision without authority is how men are owned. When he somehow lands in survival mode and stays there, he's either agreed to it or not been willing to sacrifice today for tomorrow.

If appetite outruns authority, there will be damage. If urgency precedes discernment, there will be bondage. When relief replaces governance there will be regret. The man who asks only for provision will sit at any table. The man who asks about authority chooses his seat—or leaves.

This keeps happening, because authority doesn't feel like food, doesn't feel like shelter, doesn't feel like relief. Authority feels abstract until the moment you need access. So, people sacrifice future passage to survive present pressure. That's not stupidity; that's ungoverned hunger. That's survival hunger and man is not even supposed to be in survival mode; he's the top of the food chain.

Authority was never meant to be consumed to solve survival — it was meant to grant access beyond it. We keep burning passports to stay warm, or eating them because we are hungry right now, and then wondering why we can't leave.

You are not poor; none of us are. We have to be sure that we are not eating what we shouldn't eat and that we are not misusing what we were given.

PSALM 23, REWRITTEN

The wipe is Mercy and Judgment. When God wipes a table clean, He is doing two things at once. To the righteous, He is removing confusion, ending doublemindedness and double messages. He is restoring clarity and Peace. To the adversarial, God is ending leverage over His own. He is canceling advantage over you and removing access to you by also removing proximity.

Now your keen discernment must kick in: Just because God allowed you to sit at a table doesn't mean that He approves of it. Sometimes God allows you to **see** the table to see what you will do. Sometimes God is testing the others at the table – before He righteously judges. Sometimes He is evaluating His own for promotion.

Sometimes He allows you to see the table to teach you, so you'll recognize it, when He flips it. **The** reset always changes the seating. After the wipe: Some who were at the table originally are no longer invited. Some lose proximity. Some are reassigned permanently. And the host does not explain Himself; He is God.

You prepare a table before me in the presence of my enemies... means: I will eat. I will still be provided for even in this adversarial situation. It speaks to a level of knowledge of God and trust in Him that those in relationship with Him have It means I will dine and food is not even an issue. They will watch. You want to do things to me or against me, but the LORD is with me; you can't touch me. And if the table turns hostile. The Lord who is my buckler, not my butler will clear it.

When the table has been set against you, God doesn't fix the seating, He wipes the table and starts over. The tables God set: Melchizedek & Abraham. Sustaining Wilderness manna. Mephibosheth can dine with David? The table in the Upper Room He did set, but it was a trap, when perhaps the enemy from Psalm 23 waxed bold enough to sir at the Lord's table.

When the tables are turned against you.... then we will be a resolution from the Lord; stay faithful.

He prepares a table before me: Psalm 23 gives us the principle, but Scripture gives us the case law. God is very clear about which tables He sets and which tables He allows but does not endorse.

TABLES GOD SET

God-set tables are Heaven-Initiated, Sustaining, and Covenant-Sealing.

Melchizedek & Abraham — The Table of Recognition. The first divine table in Scripture is not a feast of excess, but of **alignment**. Bread and wine are brought out. No bargaining, manipulation, future leverage, or trickery.

This table **confirms identity and victory**, not control. You are invited because of whose you are, not just because you are hungry. This is an invitation of honor.

Abraham is not diminished by the table with Melchizedek, he is **recognized** at it. The same applies to you: if you are being acknowledged and respected, by your godly identity at a table, this is a God-set table.

Wilderness Manna — The Table of Sustenance. This is not a table you choose. It is a table God **imposes** to keep you alive. Daily provision. No hoarding. If hoarding had been allowed, you all know somebody would be out early in the morning getting all they could and then reselling it in their own

Wilderness Corner Store. Like they scalp tickets. The wilderness table teaches trust, not taste. This table is temporary, but it is faithful. God sets it because nothing else was safe yet in the Wilderness.

Mephibosheth at David's Table — The Table of Restoration. This table is radical. GOD set it. Mephibosheth does not earn it. He cannot physically posture for it. He brings no value by the world's metrics, yet David seats him, permanently and publicly -- as family. This is the table where shame is hidden and brokenness is covered by proximity to the king.

God set this table. He prepares a table for me, and He restores my soul are in the very same psalm. We serve a God of Restoration. Jesus set many tables. He fed multitudes; those are God-set tables.

The Upper Room — A God-Set Table That Became a Trap. Yes, Jesus set this table. But something unprecedented happens. The enemy from Psalm 23 does not just *watch* anymore. He sits boldly at the table.

Judas crosses a line no enemy had crossed before. This is either boldness or desperation by the enemy – or both. The enemy assumes proximity equals permission. But even a fox can sneak in through a gate, it doesn't mean that fox is invited into the chicken coop. Or that he has tricked JESUS. Maybe judas thinks that seating equals authority, or that access equals control

t does not.

TABLES GOD DID NOT SET

There are tables God did not set. Jezebel's table for example is the **counterfeit answer** to Psalm 23. It looks like provision. It feels like security. It operates under royal authority. But it is **not Heaven-initiated**.

Jezebel & Ahab — The Table of Compromise. Scripture tells us that Jezebel fed the prophets of Baal and Asherah at her table. This is not hospitality. This is evil alliance and patronage. The food came with silence. The food was defiling and initiated those prophets and kept them indebted to evil. Protection required their loyalty. The seat required their submission. This table sustained false prophecy and starved the true one.

A table can feed, but when you are at a table not set by God, consider what is on that table. What is before you may not do you any good and it might even do you harm. Provision alone is not proof of approval. Just because something is good to the flesh doesn't mean it's good for the soul or the spirit of man. Jezebel's prophets ate well but God wasn't in that.

Elijah hid by a brook and was fed by a dirty bird. and yet one table collapsed overnight, while the other outlived an entire drought.

Psalm 23 versus Jezebel's Table. Psalm 23: when God prepares the table, enemies may watch, but Authority remains with the Host. At Jezebel's table: The enemy prepares the table. Authority is exchanged for access.

When the tables are set against you, or if they started out right and are now turned or stacked against you, know that God either didn't set this table, or He is allowing it for some reason. A table has turned against you when you must mute truth to remain seated. Provision is currency for your obedience. Survival is used to justify compromise. Leaving the table feels like death, but staying guarantees it; that is Jezebel's system.

God does not redeem Jezebel's table. He does not cleanse it. He does not negotiate reform. He ends it. The prophets are exposed. The drought intensifies. The table loses relevance. Jezebel's influence is ultimately destroyed. God never resets enemy-built tables. He removes His people from them.

Compared with the Upper Room at Jezebel's table, God says *"Come out."* In the Upper Room, God says *"Stay, and I will resolve it."* One table was never His. The other one Jesus set, but it became hostile. Discernment is knowing the difference.

God does not bless Jezebel's table — even when it feeds prophets. False prophets have gone out into the world and they are hosting tables all the time.

If God didn't set the table, He will not preserve it.

THE KING's DAINTIES

Do not desire the king's dainties; appetite is how hostile tables keep you seated. That means appetite for anything of this world, not just food.

Have you ever been fasting and enjoyed clarity of thoughts and clarity of hearing the voice of God, but as soon as you start eating again, it's like you can't even hear God like you used to? This is true of any food when you should be walking past that table, but it is especially true of defiled, initiating food. It is true of illegal gain, illegal power, evil shortcuts and desire for fame and quick riches.

If you must desire whatever is at this table to stay, it was never your table. This is not just about food. It is about discernment at hostile tables. From the Book of Proverbs:

When you sit to eat with a ruler, consider carefully what is before you...Do not desire his delicacies, for they are deceptive food. (Proverbs 23:1–3)

In life, you will be invited to evil tables that don't look evil. You may be invited to counterfeit tables, even to tables that look nice, seem so legit, and that start out right but they can turn. You will be seated. The table will look generous. The host will appear powerful – but are you supposed to be there? Tables can look nice, seem nice, start out right but they can turn, and become like pretty cheese in a trap.

The danger is not so much poison in the food. The danger is the <u>terms</u> attached to the meal. *Do not desire the king's dainties.* Because once you crave what the king controls, you stop asking, Who set the table?

Judas desired silver, position, and closeness to power. Judas sat at Jesus' table but was already eating from another king's menu. That is how the table turned against the Lord. Jesus hadn't lost authority, but the enemy smuggled appetite into the room.

God prepares the table. Proverbs 23 warns: *Not every table prepared before you is from God.* Both are true. So, the discernment question becomes: Who benefits if I stay hungry for this table? If you must desire it to stay, it was never your table.

So, I saw the vision of the Lord overturning the tables that are trying to overturn you.

Lord, not this time. Do not let the enemy of my soul set evil tables for me, not this month, not this year--- in the Name of Jesus.

GOD RESETS THE TABLE

Joseph went from prison rations to Pharaoh's table. This was **Table Reset Through Elevation.** Joseph is betrayed, sold, imprisoned — every table is set *against* him. Then in one day, God wipes the table clean. From the prison to the palace. From wearing chains to wearing a signet ring. Joseph went from rations to wielding the authority to feed nations. Joseph does not negotiate his old table. God removes him from it entirely.

You shall be over my house, and all my people shall be ruled according to your word.(Genesis 41).

Some of you are getting promotions sooner than you think. Lord, if that is what I need, do for me, what You did for Joseph, in the Name of Jesus. Amen.

God ends Saul's table and sets another for David. This is **Table Reset Through Separation**. David eats at Saul's table, but the table turned hostile toward David. Spears are thrown. Trust is broken. Favor becomes threat. Many are the wounds of a friend/ or a fake friend. God does not teach David how to survive Saul's table. He ends it. David flee, not in failure, but in preservation. David preserved his authority by not disrespecting the anointing on Saul. A man can expend or give up his own authority by more than sin, sex, eating; he can give it by operating in works of the flesh.

God later sets a new table: kingship.

The Lord has sought out a man after His own heart.
(1 Samuel 13)

The table reset required distance, not endurance. Lord, if that is what I need; do for me, what you did for David, in the Name of Jesus. Amen.

Elijah rejected Jezebel's table, but God Set a table for Elijah in the Wilderness. **Table Reset Through Divine Provision.** God refuses Jezebel's table for His prophet and creates one where none should exist.

I have commanded the ravens to feed you there. (1 Kings 17)

Jezebel feeds prophets. Elijah is fed by ravens. That looks backward, until it doesn't. The prophet was fed at the Brook Cherith. The widow woman of Zarephath fed him. Elijah enjoyed supernatural provision. The man who reaches for God in obedience and in sincerity will touch the Divine. When the Divine touches that man, he will never lack again, never want again. He will never hurt or be lost again. That is when that man becomes a **son** of God.

God would rather invent a table than let you stay at the wrong one. Lord, if that is what I need, do for me, what You did for Elijah, in the Name of Jesus.

Mephibosheth came all the way from Lodabar to the King's Table is one **Reset Through Restoration**. Mephibosheth lives in obscurity with no table, and no future. God moved the heart of the King for Mephibosheth. David resets everything from location to identity, to access, and permanence.

> You shall eat bread at my table continually. (2 Samuel 9)

Lord, if that is what I need, do for me, what You did for Mephibosheth, in the Name of Jesus.

From the Upper Room **Table** of **Betrayal** to the Resurrection, we see the ultimate table reset. The Upper Room becomes hostile. Betrayal enters. Satan entered the betrayer. The table turns. So, God ends that table forever. After the Resurrection, Jesus sets a new table, for us.

At the Shoreline Meal, there was bread and fish. There was no Judas, no money, no coins, no bargaining and no pricing. But there was restoration; just restoration.

> Jesus took the bread and gave it to them, and likewise the fish. (John 21)

This is the reset table.

Lord, if that is what I need, do for me what You did for Your Disciples, in the Name of Jesus.

When a table turns against you, God chooses one of three responses. Either He will remove you, remove them, or remove the whole table itself. But God never leaves His people eating under hostile terms.

PSALM 23 — NOW FULLY RESOLVED

You prepare a table before me in the presence of my enemies…" Thank You, Lord, I will eat when You set it. I will sit when You have set it. Holy Spirit, help me discern every table. I will walk past tables that I should walk past and from tables that don't deserve my presence. I will leave every table when You clear it, and I trust You to prepare what comes next.

When God resets the table, it is not punishment — it is proof that the old arrangement has expired.

The ultimate table reset is the communion table, where appetite is re-ordered, allegiance is restored, and governance is returned to Christ. At this table, we do not take control; we receive covenant.

Communion is God's table reset. it is remembering the Lord's death until He returns. It is remembering covenant with the Lord, covenant received and authority restored. It is when all things are set back in order.

WARFARE PRAYERS

I break, every trap of wickedness set against me at any table that I happen upon, or that I am called to, or summoned to, in the Name of Jesus. I render every trick and trap null and void, in the Name of Jesus.

I reject every morsel of the king's dainties. I reject every morsel of contaminated, defiled or corruption masquerading as food, in the Name of Jesus.

I reject and release all defiled food or beverage of evil initiation or evil covenantal agreement, in the Name of Jesus. I break every evil agreement and covenant made by food or beverage of any kind, in the name of Jesus.

Every predetermined assigned seat of danger, mischief or loss, I refuse. I refuse it, in the Name of Jesus. I refuse the seat of the scornful, in the Name of Jesus.

Every rigged table, every table with predetermined outcomes, I reverse your planned outcomes, and I receive the good. My enemies, what you had for me, you have it, in the Name of Jesus.

Every negotiating or bargaining table with hidden prices, hidden costs or already agreed upon terms that do not honor me, but instead they are there to steal from me, I reject that table, I condemn that table, and your evil negotiations, in the Name of Jesus.

Every table of Trickery Deception, Lies, fall down, be overturned, be destroyed and burned to ashes, in the Name of Jesus.

Every table of defilement or evil initiation or evil covenant, be destroyed, in the Name of Jesus.

Lord, sharpen my discernment so that I miss nothing, in the Name of Jesus.

Amen.

PROPHETIC PRAYER

Father God,

You are the One who prepares tables and the One who clears them. You are not confused by proximity, nor threatened by presence. You see every table that has been set before me, and every table that has been set *against* me.

In the Name of Jesus Christ,

I renounce every appetite that tied me to any wrong table-- ever.

I renounce every sin, transgression and iniquity that has dragged me to the wrong table. Lord, forgive, have Mercy on me and remember my iniquity and the iniquity of my ancestors no more, in the Name of Jesus.

Every desire that kept me seated longer than obedience required at any table of any kind, whether it is a bargaining table, a dinner table, or any table of any category, in the Name of Jesus.

We move through life from table to table, Lord keep me from tables that are in place to steal, kill, destroy, or to govern my soul, in the Name of Jesus.

Lord, let every craving for approval, provision, proximity, or power that did not come from You be canceled, in the Name of Jesus.

Lord, Where I ate in good faith and it was sweet to the taste, but was bitter in my belly, Lord remove all bitterness and heal me, in the Name of Jesus.

Where after sitting down at the table I later discovered the table had turned hostile. **Lord, I do not condemn myself – Father, I release the table. Take Your authority, Lord – remember Your covenant with us and reign, in the Name of Jesus.**

Father, **wipe clean what has been turned against .me.** Invalidate corrupt agreements. Reverse evil judgments against us. Cancel silent expectations. Expose hidden terms. Break dark covenants I may have made unknowingly, in the Name of Jesus.

Where access was mistaken for alignment, where proximity was mistaken for permission, where seating was mistaken for authority — LORD **reset me; in the Name of Jesus.**

By your Grace and Mercy give me Divine reset when the table has been set against me, or when the table has turned against me, in the Name of Jesus.

Lord, for those who are fasting in this season: Lord, let their sacrifice sharpen discernment, not fear. Let abstinence clarify authority, not augment anxiety, in the Name of Jesus.

And for those who are not fasting: Father, teach them that fasting is not only about food, it is about refusing whatever feeds the wrong future, in the Name of Jesus.

Prepare the table You intend to sustain me with now. The table that carries peace, clarity, truth, strength, and freedom from all manipulation, in the Name of Jesus.

When the table is corrupt: If You must remove me — Lord, thank You for the anointing to get up and go – to leave, in the Name of Jesus.

When the table is contaminated: If You must remove them, remove them. Thank You, Lord. When the table is defiled: If You must overturn the table, have Your way Lord, in Jesus' Name.

When the table is a trap: If you must remove the table itself — remove it without regret, in the Name of Jesus.

I trust You with the reset. The Lord is my shepherd, I shall not want: He prepares a table before me, in the Presence of mine enemies, in the Name of Jesus.

And when my enemies are present, let them see me nourished, let them see Your Glory. Let them see me calm, seated, assured, fed, and strong, and in my proper authority, in the Name of Jesus.

Lord, I will not desire the king's dainties. I will not eat deceptive bread, nor bread of initiation, defilement, affliction or sorrows. Evermore, Lord give us that bread; the Break of Heaven, the Bread of life.

We will not drink from defiling cups of unrighteousness. Lord give me an overflowing cup of Joy, Peace, abundance, health, healing, wisdom, knowledge, understanding divine guidance, divine opportunities, in the Name of Jesus.

Father, I will wait for what You prepare. In Jesus' Name.
Amen.

WHEN DOVES FLY

That year, in the Holy Land there were two buses in our tour group. We went to a place that was "like" the Upper Room because scholars don't know exactly where it was/is. When we drove up, doves flew out everywhere. We wondered if it was scripted --- it was so dramatic.

What we witnessed fits Scripture with unsettling precision. When we approached the place associated with the Upper Room — a space of Table, Bread, Betrayal, Covenant, reset, doves flew out.

Doves in Scripture are not decoration. They are markers of transition. At Jesus' baptism, the dove marks Heaven opening. In the temple, doves were the offering of the poor — and the very thing Jesus released when He overturned the tables. In the Upper Room arc, what happens next is departure: Judas leaves, Jesus leaves, the table ends, the Spirit comes later.

Doves flying *out* is not about arrival. It's about release and evacuation. They flew out everywhere. That's not peace imagery, that's movement imagery. It says, *"This season does not stay contained." "What was held here has already moved on."*

When a table turns hostile, God doesn't renovate the room, He clears it.

We weren't just visiting a site; we were standing at the junction of a table that ended, a betrayal that was permitted, a covenant that was completed elsewhere, and a Spirit that would no longer be confined to rooms. The doves didn't descend; they ascended and then departed. That's not Pentecost. That's closure before reset.

Even the doves knew the table had already ended. *This season does not stay contained. What was held here has already moved on.*

When a table turns hostile, God doesn't renovate the room; He clears it.

We were standing at the junction of a table that ended. A betrayal that was permitted. A covenant that was completed elsewhere. And a Spirit that would no longer be confined to rooms. Some moments aren't loud — they're aligned. And alignment always feels dramatic to people who know Scripture.

Even the doves (creation) knew the table had already ended." When Jesus was born, were the animals shocked? No. Creation knows. Creation gets it. Were the stars surprised? No. The Heavens? The table is never singular in its effect. It reveals, divides, seals, and resets — all at once.

At the table, bread is offered, covenant is extended, betrayal is exposed, peace is proclaimed, authority is clarified. But, not everyone responds the same way.

Covenant always produces divergence. Whenever covenant is offered, response is revealed. At Jesus' table, some receive, some waver, some deny, some betray. This is not failure of the table; it is the *function* of the table. Light does not create division it reveals it. So, while some are making covenant with the Lord, others are rejecting it at the very same table.

That is consistent from Eden forward.

Jesus reestablishes Peace for the Earth Itself. Through Jesus Christ, covenant is not merely personal. It is cosmic.

As the Son of God, Jesus does what Adam could not and Noah prefigured. He restores Peace between Heaven and Earth. He reopens the question: *Is there now a resting place for Peace?* The imagery of doves flying out echoes Noah sending the dove from the ark, not to judge, but to search, to see whether Peace could land again, The dove is not sent to condemn the earth, it is sent to test whether the Earth can now receive rest.

That's covenant language.

Doves matter. They signify Peace, the Spirit, purity, rest, and reconciliation. Their movement outward says something unmistakable. Peace has been reoffered. The question now is not whether Heaven is willing, but whether the Earth will receive it.

The moment felt scripted, but it wasn't choreography, it was theology made visible.

For the earnest expectation of the creature waiteth
for the manifestation of the sons of God.
(Romans 8:19)

Creature here means *creation, that is all that God made.* Creation is waiting for the sons of God to appear as who they are. They need to appear as fully grown sons of God that God can be well-pleased in. They should be walking in proper authority, revealed, not driven by appetite for the flesh or things of this world. Creation is stuck in frustration because governance is delayed until sons mature enough to steward it.

At the table, covenant is offered to all, but Peace only rests where it is received. The doves were sent out to see if Peace had a place to land again because once the land is healed, Creation will have a place to rest. Creation having rest is a test of the sons of God being in proper authority and vice versa each bearing witness of the other.

WHEN TABLES TURN

When the tables are turned against you… you need the Lord. You need Him at that table. Call on the Lord. When even a God-initiated space becomes hostile, when what once nourished begins to poison we need God. When what was safe becomes strategic for the enemy, we need the Presence of the Lord to quash the presence of the enemy.

We all need discernment to know what table, where, when, IF – and also if something changes.

When tables turn against you, God will resolve the issue. Sometimes by wiping the table clean. Sometimes by ending the season entirely. Sometimes by removing you before collapse. Or, allowing betrayal to surface so it can no longer operate covertly against you.

The Upper Room led to the Cross, and the Cross ended the plans of that *table* forever. Amen. No more bargaining. No more pricing. No more hidden coins.

There are tables God did not set (though He may have allowed them. Here is where discernment is required.

Psalm 23, Now Fully Interpreted. "You prepare a table before me in the presence of my enemies..." This means, I will know which tables are Yours. I will not sit at every table. I will not dine at every table. I will not negotiate at every table. I will recognize when a table turns hostile. And I trust You, LORD to resolve what I cannot fix.

When the tables are turned against you, God does not salvage the setting. He brings resolution, even if it costs the whole table.

At the table, there is no food fight. This is not a food fight; this is a fight for the righteous. The overturning of the tables in the Temple wasn't about tables and coins. It was about who had the right to mediate access to God. This is not a food fight. This is not a food fight this is a righteous confrontation. A *food fight* is childish, reactive, messy, pointless. What Jesus does is measured, targeted, and righteous. He doesn't throw food; He overturns systems. He doesn't lash out; He reclaims what was consecrated.

This wasn't about tables and coins. It was about who had the right to mediate access to God. That's why Merchants scatter, Doves fly. Coins expose ownership and motives, and no one dares stop Him.

Righteousness had entered the room.

In the Book of Job 1, we're told something very specific *before* the wind came. Job's sons were feasting. Each one hosted in his own house. The gatherings were cyclical. Food and wine were central. Job regularly rose early to sanctify them, *"just in case* "Scripture is showing us a pattern of distraction, not celebration.

The text does not say the children were wicked. It does not say the feast was sinful. It does not say God judged them for eating. So, I am not saying that eating causes judgment. But I am saying that the table was not fortified. There was access somewhere else the enemy could not have gotten in.

The table was vulnerable. The children were scattered (each in his own house). The father was not present. The gathering was inward-focused, not watchful. The feast had become *routine*, not reverent. *"A great wind came from across the wilderness and struck the four corners of the house...* This was not an attack on food. It was an attack on unguarded atmosphere.

Food can distract when discernment is required. That's exactly why fasting shows up before major transitions in Scripture. Not because food is evil, but because appetite softens vigilance. The fall of Sodom and Gomorrah started with food.

Job's children were not sinning, but they were unguarded, even though Job was sacrificing for them regularly. The acts of man—religion, the old sacrifice… The table wasn't wicked, but it wasn't watchful either. And when the wind came, the table could not protect them.

This also explains why Job fasted and sacrificed for his children. Job's children were behaving more like the 'children of men' than sons of God. They were letting daddy handle their spiritual needs when they were old enough to be doing it themselves. How do I know? They had their own houses and they had spouses; they were old enough. Yet, Job instinctively knew Joy needs covering. Celebration needs sanctification. Tables need spiritual authority, not just abundance.

Food doesn't invite danger, but distraction can. Not every table is sinful, but not every table is fortified.

A table can easily become a distraction. A man's gotta eat, but attention to spiritual matters, matters. Scripture shows us moments when the table itself isn't sinful, but it becomes distracting. And when vigilance is lowered, even good gatherings can become vulnerable. Job's children were not rebelling; they were feasting. Well, if the feast wasn't unto the Lord, who was it *unto*? Remember, no table is neutral. If it is not dedicated, spiritual opportunists will insist or sneak their way in.

Scripture makes a point to tell us that not because food was evil, but because attention was inward, scattered, and unguarded when the wind came.

Sometimes God resets a table not because it's corrupt, but because it's distracting us from what requires watchfulness. Distraction is not rebellion — but it is vulnerability. What feeds you should never dull you. Strong beverage? What is to refresh you, should never enmesh you.

FULL SEASONS

Biblically,. 40 marks a full season of divine process *long enough for exposure, transformation, or decision to occur*. Forty marks the time required for God's purpose to mature. Biblically, forty is completion of process, not excess of time.

Not rushed. Not indefinite--, but, enough.

Scriptural patterns that prove this follow.

Moses was 40 days on Mount Sinai. There, there was identity formation, law, covenant transfer. The time wasn't arbitrary; it was sufficient for revelation.

Elijah took 40 days' journey to Horeb. There old exhaustion burned off, new instruction was received. It took *exactly as long as it took*.

Jesus spent 40 days in the wilderness There, temptation was exhausted, authority clarified, ministry launched. Not a hunger stunt, but a threshold crossing.

In the Book of Jonah, we learn of the 40 days warning to Nineveh. Time allotted for repentance, but not endless, not instant. God gave them enough time to respond.

The Book of Genesis recounts 40 days of rain in the flood. This was enough rain and flooding to dismantle the old system completely. This was total reset.

So, what does "40" really communicate? Biblically, it says, *This season will last until its purpose is fulfilled.* It is long enough for exposure. Long enough for resistance to surface. Long enough for obedience to be tested. Long enough for God to finish what He intends, but not longer than necessary.

Some revelations need time, not volume. Some seasons don't end because we're tired; they end because they're complete. God does not rush formation, but He does close cycles. Just like tables, just like resets, just like fasting.

Jesus learned everything about tables. He got "table education by turning down 40 days of tables. The Education of Authority. Before Jesus ever sat at tables with sinners, rulers, Pharisees, disciples, or betrayers…
He learned how to refuse them. That happens in the wilderness.

Jesus learned authority over tables by living without them. You cannot govern tables you have never learned to live without. You cannot govern tables that are already governing you. How you interact with money --- determines if you will dominate money or if it will dominate you. God is looking.

This shifts the issue from *food* to authority. It removes shame and exposes structure. It explains why fasting clarifies leadership. It explains why some people can't leave certain systems. It explains why Jesus had to refuse tables *before* confronting them. And it fits perfectly with the 40-day wilderness frame:

Jesus wasn't proving endurance. He was breaking **governance**. By the time He returns hunger no longer commands Him. Bread no longer tempts Him. Systems no longer leverage Him. So, when He enters the temple, He is free enough to overturn tables, because none of them own Him.

God gave Adam and Eve authority (governance) over everything He created, but they let themselves be overtaken by the tree? through its *fruit*? God gave Adam and Eve governance over creation, but they surrendered authority by submitting to what they were meant to govern.

Adam and Eve were given authority over every created thing, but they allowed the tree, through its fruit, to govern their decision instead. Since they were getting the knowledge of good and evil—not having been told, according to the text that they were trading anything, shouldn't they have been wiser, if they were getting 'knowledge' in this transaction?

But we learned later that it is not knowledge from above.... After all, the devil didn't have anything of God's that he could give a human.

When they were discernment-focused, they were assigned dominion, but they deferred discernment. What they were meant to oversee, they allowed to overtake them when they became appetite-focused.

They were created to govern the garden, but appetite redirected their authority. Submission-Focused (Very Precise Theologically).

"Their fall was not the loss of authority, but the misplacement of submission."

God gave Adam and Eve authority over every tree—but the moment they let the fruit govern them, they forfeited the ground they were meant to rule."

-- that's the same thing Esau did...appetite made him give up his position/authority/birthright. When it came to appetite versus authority, Adam lost. Esau lost. Judas lost. Jesus did not give in; Jesus maintained authority.

Esau is the example of: When Appetite Trades Authority. Scripture tells us that Esau did not lose his birthright through violence, deception, or weakness; he traded it. He exchanged it, for stew. Not because stew was powerful, but because appetite was urgent. *"Thus Esau despised his birthright."* Book of Genesis 25.

That word *despised* doesn't mean hatred. It means to treat as insignificant under pressure. Esau let hunger reframe value. This Is the same inversion as Eden. Adam and Eve were meant to govern the tree. Esau was meant to govern his appetite. Judas was meant to guard proximity. Jesus was tempted to satisfy hunger apart from the Father. Same test. Different responses.

Appetite doesn't remove authority. It rushes decisions until authority is surrendered willingly. That's why Scripture never portrays Esau as tricked. He was hungry, not deceived.

You cannot govern what you allow to govern you. Esau didn't lose his birthright. He priced it under appetite.

ISCARIOT

Just like Judas priced Jesus, the moneychangers priced worship. Jezebel priced prophecy. **Contrast: Jesus in the Wilderness**

Esau says, "I am about to die; what good is my birthright?"

Jesus says, "Man does not live by bread alone." One trades inheritance for food. The other preserves inheritance by refusing it. That's not fasting as discipline or punishment, it's fasting as governance training.

Esau fell because appetite made authority feel optional. Esau traded his authority; it wasn't stolen. (The blessing was stolen, but not the birthright.) With Esau, Scripture says something devastatingly calm: "Thus Esau despised his birthright." He wasn't tricked.
He wasn't coerced. He wasn't ignorant. He priced what was sacred under appetite.

Hebrews later says he sought repentance "with tears but could not recover what he had already transferred. That doesn't mean God hated him. It means governance once traded is not easily reclaimed.

This makes the reset harder. When governance is willingly given away Discernment dulls, Conviction weakens, Justification increases. Appetite becomes the new authority. At that point, the problem isn't access to Mercy. It's desire for governance. God does not override the will to rule us *for us*.

Judas sopped in the same plate as Jesus. Judas would eat from the one that was feeding him and still betray Him. That is cold blooded.

Jesus says, "It is the one to whom I give this piece of bread when I have dipped it in the dish."
(John 13:26)

That detail matters. In the ancient world, sopping from the same dish was not casual eating, it was serious intimacy. It meant trust, friendship, even a shared life. And Judas Iscariot participates fully. He eats what Jesus provides. He receives what Jesus offers. He stays close enough to share the plate.

And still Judas betrays Him. Evil men are stupid enough not to recognize Grace. Evil men are not wise or aware enough to know that people can <u>see</u> the mess they are doing, but if they say nothing at first, or even for a while, they are giving the perpetrator enough Grace to get it together. They are giving time for them to at least stop even if the offender doesn't repent or ask for forgiveness.

But to be fed either physically or spiritually by a person and still betray Him—that's cold. That perpetrator is not ignorant, they have divided allegiance.

This is so sobering.

Judas shows us something unsettling but true: It is possible to eat from the same source and live from a different loyalty. He was nourished by Jesus' presence. but governed by another appetite. This is not hunger. This is duplicity.

Adam ate fruit while standing in God's garden. Esau ate stew while standing in his inheritance. Judas ate bread while standing next to Christ. In every case Eating did not equal allegiance.

Which brings us right back to your governing axiom: You cannot govern tables that are already governing you.

Judas didn't betray because he lacked access. He betrayed because access did not rule him. Judas ate from the hand of Jesus while already feeding another allegiance. "Proximity does not cure betrayal. Enemies are members of your own household.

Because the real danger isn't *being near the table*. The danger is letting the table feed you while something else governs you. This, alone explains *why* Jesus had to reset the table entirely.

If a man has willingly given up governance (authority) is the reset more difficult? Judas didn't recover. Esau didn't recover. the rest of us have at least a hope in Christ.

Voluntary surrender of governance makes a reset harder, but not impossible — and Christ is the dividing line. Governance Given Away vs. Governance Interrupted or hijacked is different. Scripture distinguishes between:

1. Authority lost through deception, weakness, or immaturity

2. Authority surrendered knowingly, repeatedly, and willfully

The second carries greater consequence, because the person has reassigned allegiance. Judas: willingly reassigned governance. Judas was not deceived about who Jesus was. He was not excluded. He was not starving. He was not ignorant of consequence, yet Judas chose to betray the Lord.

John's Gospel shows that *after* he receives the bread, Satan enters him (John 13:27). That is not temptation; that is yielded governance. Judas didn't merely fail, he handed authority over and then acted from that place.

That's why repentance does not restore him He regrets the outcome. But never reassigns governance back to God. He tries to *undo the consequence*, not *return allegiance.*

That's why repentance does not restore him. He regrets the outcome, but never reassigns governance back to God. He tries to undo the consequence, not return allegiance. This is why with figures like Esau, Saul, and even Judas regretted loss, grieved consequence, and wanted reversal. But they did not return authority, surrender governance, yield appetite, restore allegiance. W*orldly sorrow still only leads to more grief and eventually* death. G*odly sorrow* leads to repentance unto life

True repentance is the reassignment of authority, lordship back to God. David doesn't ask first for relief. He asks for realignment.

A Prayer of Repentance, Renunciation, and Reassignment of Governance

Father God,
I come to You without excuse and without
negotiation.

I acknowledge that where appetite ruled,
authority was displaced.

I do not come asking You to undo consequences.
I come asking You to **restore governance**.

Where I chose relief over obedience,
I repent.

Where I consumed what should have been governed,
I repent.

Where I remained seated at tables You did not host,
I repent.

I renounce every agreement made with appetite, fear,
urgency, or desire
that replaced allegiance to You.

Cleanse me — not only from the act,
but from the *inclination* that led to it.

Create in me a clean heart, O God,
and renew a right spirit within me —
a spirit that can be trusted with authority.

Restore to me the joy of Your salvation,
not so I may feel better,
but so I may walk rightly.

I return governance to You now.
My appetite does not rule me.
My emotions do not rule me.
My urgency does not rule me.

You do.

In Jesus' name,
Amen.

Repentance is not regret over loss; it is the return of governance.

HOPE IN CHRIST

Unlike Judas or Esau, we live on this side of the Cross. In Jesus Christ, authority can be restored, not just protected. Governance can be relearned. Appetite can be retrained. Allegiance can be reassigned.

Peter denied Jesus knowingly — and was restored.

Why?

Because Peter returned allegiance, submitted governance. Accepted reformation, not just relief. The resurrection creates a category Judas never entered re-governed life.

So the Balanced, Biblical Answer Is This

You might say it this way (clean and sober):

When governance is willingly surrendered, reset becomes harder — but in Christ, it is not impossible. God can reset what was broken by weakness more easily than what was traded by allegiance — but Christ makes restoration possible where it would otherwise be final.

This teaching should never be used to declare, "That person is beyond hope." "You've gone too far." "God is done with you." Scripture does not authorize us to make those judgments. What it *does* authorize is this warning. Don't let appetite decide what only governance should.

The danger is not failure — it is transferring authority to what cannot restore you. You're not teaching despair here. You're teaching responsibility with hope. And you're right *the rest of us have hope in Christ* because He restores governance, not just forgiveness.

THEIR BELLIES ARE THEIR GODS

Ungoverned Hunger

For many walk… whose god is their belly, and whose glory is in their shame, who mind earthly things. The phrase comes directly from Epistle to the Philippians 3:18–19.

Paul is not talking about overeating. He is talking about governance.

This chapter is not about food, it's about what gets obeyed first. "The belly" in Scripture represents appetite, urgency, comfort-seeking, immediate relief, demand for satisfaction *now.* To say *"their bellies are their gods"* means appetite has replaced authority. In Eden, they decided to ignore or forget about authority and assuage their "hunger." We don't know if Esau had low blood sugar or not, but he sincerely believed his need for food was urgent. He even thought that he might die if he did not eat. Considering the wealth of Abraham, the wealth of their father, Isaac, these boys were not brought up poor or lacking, so Esau's behavior was very uncool and not appropriate for his station in life.

Judas craved power or to be power-adjacent or to just get in wherever he could get in. He may or may not have listened when Jesus taught, he held the money bag and he obviously wanted more so he arranged to sell Jesus. This was totally demonic as only the dark kingdom deals in buying and selling men and the souls of men. (Revelations 13)

Jezebel hungered for power and she also being the *spirit* of a witch got her 'powers' from the dark kingdom. She owned prophets and they all dealt in false prophecy.

Tables that turn hostile are only hostile if that is not what the table guest wants. Sometimes when the table turns dark that is exactly what the guest wants. And why? Because their appetite is about to be fed or at least attended to. Depending on the level of appetite some people are desperate and as long as they get what they want, they do not care how. By any means necessary is a mantra of too many. A table only feels hostile when it stops serving what the guest came for.

Jesus refused bread in the wilderness because His belly did not govern His life or His choices.

Who is supplying what at the at the table is why tables must be discerned, not merely enjoyed. Resets are sometimes severe. When appetite governs decision-making, even sacred things become negotiable. When the table or whoever is hosting the table assesses the guest and their level of desire or desperation they may decide that anything goes and the guest who has no self-governance may go for just anything.

Appetite is now, immediate, urgent so the voice that a man may be listening to will be leading him into flesh acts and acts based on flesh needs and desires. Those of higher estate, those governed by authority behave much differently.

You cannot govern tables that are already governing you so this is why we expect more from people of high estate and of high authority.

TURNING TABLES

Adele's song, *Turning Tables* is not about anger or drama. Nor is it about a place to spin vinyl. It's about regaining governance in a relationship where power has been reversed. At its core, the song is about this moment *"I'm no longer eating at a table that silences me."*

The central theme of ***Turning Tables.*** The song describes A relationship where one person controls the emotional environment. Conversations that are rigged. Outcomes that are predetermined. Vulnerability is used as leverage. That's a **hostile table**. The speaker realizes that the table is no longer safe. Truth is punished. Silence is demanded. Staying requires self-erasure. So, she says, in essence *"I'm flipping this arrangement."* Not to dominate but to **stop being dominated**.

Adele isn't talking about food. She's talking about **terms**. The table became **governing. Normal human a**ppetite for peace, approval, and love kept her seated. Emotional hunger replaced authority; even desiring normal human things is appetite and the manipulator will use it. In the song, discernment finally interrupts endurance.

The one who stays in a connection like that is modeling **ungoverned hunger** in relational form.

When she says, *I won't let you close enough to hurt me*, is the moment that she is removing access, resetting proximity, and reclaiming governance. This mirrors David leaving Saul's table. Jesus overturning temple tables. Walking away when the table turns hostile.

The dynamic we've been discussing throughout this book is real. It is not just Biblical; it's human. This example shows that even in the natural, people can intuitively recognize **table inversion**. And we can see that what God put in Scripture is for our real life.

Adele and her beautiful voice and her moving songs are not theology, they shouldn't be moved into church settings, but I wanted to share how discernment is needed in everyday life, even in relationships and if a secular song writer can see it, so should we so we can govern ourselves accordingly. *Modern language still reaches for this metaphor. When a relationship* becomes controlling, people instinctively say 'the tables have turned.' Even contemporary music captures this moment — when someone recognizes that what once felt like connection has become leverage.

Tables are not just Biblical, not just spiritual, they are in our every day lives. They are **psychological and relational.** People instinctively know when an arrangement has turned against them, so don't stay in a hostile set up too long just because it is 'spiritual', or the person hosting is authoritative, powerful, famous, or they've promised you something that they aren't even delivering. If they don't mean you any good, then discern and get up from that table.

God has given us what we need in Scripture already for a reason. You can say, "I'm ending this arrangement" without ever saying it. Just get up and leave. Or, depending on the relationship you can say, "I'm withdrawing my consent from this arrangement." "I'm no longer participating in this arrangement." This removes blame and still ends it.

"This arrangement no longer has my authority." "I'm turning this arrangement back over to its maker." Return to sender; this isn't working for me. Bye.

Other options include: "This arrangement ends here."

BUT! No matter how you say it, action is still required, else it becomes like Pilate who washed his hands but kept his seat. True discernment stands up and leaves.

Many people believe they have disengaged because they voice discomfort, express objection, or just prayed privately. But they stayed—remember your authority is with you. So if you stay, if you are present, silent, complaining and still benefiting, then Scripture does not recognize that as innocence.

Pilate said, "I'm not responsible" but he remained in his position of authority and power. Outcomes still flowed through him. Threatening to leave without leaving is handwashing, not withdrawal. This may soothe the conscience while attempting to avoid consequences.

So, at a hostile table, originally one party manipulates, the other sees it (discerns). After repeated, unacted upon threats, both parties are now negotiating or manipulating. You know manipulation is witchcraft, right? Both are applying pressure for domination or intimidation, still witchcraft. Both are trying to govern or control the table, and that is still absolutely witchcraft.

A hostile or antagonistic table cannot be healed by **mirroring its tactics**. Those who say, "Oh, I'm just matching their energy" need to think this all the way through. If their energy is witchcraft, then what are you doing?

When departure becomes a threat instead of an action, it becomes manipulation. If you're still seated, you aren't really leaving, you're still playing the game.

Leaving is not punishment. Leaving is not drama. Leaving is not manipulation. Leaving is movement of authority. Until authority moves, nothing at the table actually changes. The person who keeps threatening to leave but never leaves is still seated. Talk is cheap if you're still in your seat.

To reclaim your governance in a case like this the most powerful move is not to flip it — but to end it. Jesus appropriately flipped the table in the Temple, but God clearly knows when to completely end a table.

Discernment sharpens by use and it matures when we learn that authority is not asserted by force but authority is reclaimed by withdrawal.

THE ANOINTING TO SET A GODLY TABLE

Not every table carries covenant. The anointing to set a godly table is not common, and it is not automatic. God imparts it to a man. A covenant table is not defined by abundance, beauty, or invitation; it is defined by who has been authorized to host it.

Many tables are counterfeits. Some are distractions. Some are transactions. And some are deliberately stacked against the very ones invited to sit. That is why discernment is not optional.

Before you sit, you must ask: Who is hosting this table? And just as importantly What governs them? You will know them by their fruit not their polish, not their offerings, not their language, and certainly not their *apples*. Fruit reveals governance. Fruit reveals allegiance. Fruit reveals whether a table nourishes covenant or quietly negotiates your authority away. A Godly table strengthens obedience. A counterfeit table dulls it. And the difference is always found in the host.

Every table carries the nature of its host. Before you eat, discern who has authority to feed you. that man, the one who is dating you and invites you to dinner ... he has set a table, what will you do? Should you be there? I don't mean emotionally because he's cute or you like his bank account, but spiritually is this a person you should ever be at a table with?

Every invitation is a table. And yes —, the man who invites you to dinner has set a table. That table may look casual. It may feel romantic. It may seem harmless. But it is still a table. And every table carries intention, expectation, authority, and terms. A dinner invitation is never *just* about food. It is about **access**.

This matters (without being crude or fearful). When someone sets a table, they are doing at least three things: Establishing proximity, creating atmosphere, or positioning themselves as host. Host status matters. The host controls timing, environment, and pacing and often controls expectations. That doesn't make the invitation wrong — but it makes it revealing.

Discernment questions before you sit, wisdom asks What kind of table does this person consistently set? Does this table strengthen clarity or blur it? Does it honor boundaries or test them? Does it nourish discernment or dull it? Again — not paranoid. Just observant.

Every invitation is a table. Business, deals, transactions and exchanges are happening every day and all the time. Before you sit, you should discern not only what is being served but who believes they have authority in the room.

That's grown. That's protective. That's biblical.

If you would not submit your discernment at the table, do not submit your appetite. Dating is not just conversation; it is discernment in proximity. there are women who go on dates with men just to get a free meal..... they are only discerning (if you can call it that) if this man can afford the meal and what's in it for them, not considering what they may lose.

When appetite masquerades as discernment, it is governance inversion through appetite. There are people who sit at tables only discerning the menu and not discerning the host. This means that as soon as you receive the invitation start praying about it, don't wait until you get to the table that day unless you are really good at discerning in real time with distractions all around you.

They are not asking *Who is this person? What governs them? What does proximity to them cost me?* They are asking only *Can he afford this? What can I extract? What's in it for me right now?* That is not discernment. That is **appetite dressed up as wisdom**.

This is not harmless. The woman who chooses an extravagant restaurant for a first date not out of mutual interest, but because *"he's paying"* has already made a decision about governance. She has decided the meal is worth the potential misalignment. The moment is worth the message; the appetite outweighs the cost. What is she selling for a sandwich? Her authority? This is so Esau-like.

Scripture is very clear on this pattern. When appetite governs the decision, authority is always the price. What is lost is not money. What is lost is clarity, credibility, and self-governance.

This is still a table. Even if she has no romantic intention. Even if she believes she is "using" the situation. Even if she thinks she is in control. She is still sitting at a table she did not set, under a host she has not discerned, for a purpose she has already trivialized. That is never neutral.

When the only question we ask is what we can get, we stop asking what we might lose. Free meals are never free when they cost governance.

Modern culture normalizes transactional tables. appetite is rewarded and discernment is mocked. Appetite and desire is how people learn to value access over alignment. It's Esau with better lighting. It's Judas without thirty pieces of silver — *yet*.

If you sit at a table for extraction, do not be surprised when something is extracted from you. Turn around is fair play. The prophets who sat at Jezebel's table did her bidding.

When provision purchases allegiance. The prophets who sat at Jezebel's table did not merely eat her food, they served her will. That table was not hospitality, it was patronage. Provision came with expectation. Sustenance came with silence. And the seat came with submission. What they ate shaped what they said.

The same principle applies in quieter, modern ways. When *he* is buying the food, he may be buying more than the food. He may be buying access, tolerance, silence, patience, your alliance, the benefit of the doubt, or continued proximity. It is not always done consciously, or maliciously--, but the question remains the same.

What does the host believe the table entitles him to? Better find out. This is not about generosity. Godly provision never demands allegiance. This is about expectations disguised as kindness. When provision becomes leverage, the table is no longer neutral. And when allegiance is assumed because sustenance was supplied, the table has already begun to govern.

If that dinner host is also plying their guest with drinks--, that's sorcery. It is too easy to give up agency or governance when under the influence of anything, especially pharmakeia. So the woman who goes to dinner to trick a guy into paying for an expensive meal and he is ordering drink after drink for her… who's zooming who? It's all manipulation and that is still witchcraft.

Provision that expects allegiance is not generosity, it is control. When food purchases silence, the table has already turned. This is not suspicion; this is discernment of power dynamics. And you are restoring a truth Scripture has always held Who feeds you matters — because feeding creates influence. And, does this person even have authority through God to even set a Godly table?

Melchizedek's name means King *of Righteousness*. Melchi = king. Zedek / Tzedek = righteousness. So, *Melchizedek* literally means, "King who governs by righteousness." He is both king and priest, not appointed by lineage, not sustained by a system, hosting a covenant table (bread and wine), recognizing Abraham's authority without controlling him

This is **pure, God-authorized governance**. **Zadok is a name that means, r**ighteous or just. Zadok is the priest who remains faithful when others defect,. Later, Zadok is established permanently in the priesthood. God explicitly removes other priestly lines and confirms Zadok's line.

Why?

Because Zadok represents priesthood governed by righteousness, not appetite or politics. God entrusts tables to those governed by righteousness. Melchizedek sets a table. It's Godly because there are no evil motives. There is no leverage, no demand, no control. Zadok keeps the priesthood and there is no rebellion, no appetite for power.

Contrasting this with Jezebel's prophets—she fed them to control them. Esau was hungry and traded authority. Judas eats and then betrays. Same world; different folks, different dispensations; different choices, different governance.

The Bible quietly teaches that only the righteous can host covenant tables without corrupting them. That's why Melchizedek can feed Abraham without owning him. Zadok can serve at the altar without exploiting access. Jesus can host a table without coercion.

This also explains why counterfeit hosts always use food to extract allegiance.

Only those governed by righteousness can feed others without seeking control. Righteousness is what qualifies a host.

MAMRE

While writing this book, I kept *seeing* Abraham in Mamre entertaining those Angels. A man set that table, but he was by then considered a man of righteousness, so God ordained or authorize Abraham to set a Godly table, to be a Godly host.

At Mamre a man sets the table, but God initiates the visit (Genesis 18), Abraham is sitting at the entrance of his tent at Mamre when three visitors appear Abraham did not summon the guests. God initiates the encounter. Abraham responds with hospitality. At Mamre there is no appetite pressure. No urgency. No leverage. No distraction. No negotiation. The meal does not **govern Abraham.** Abraham governs the moment, but he is not trying to manipulate anyone or anything. Mamre is not a hostile, cautionary or even a reset table. Mamre is a **confirmation table**, not a governing one. Abraham is already aligned. Already obedient. Already circumcised in covenant. Already walking in authority. The table does not form him, it **reveals** him. In this case, the Promise is reaffirmed. Future is announced. Judgment is disclosed (Sodom). Intercession follows. This table leads to **revelation**, not temptation.

Mamre shows us. When a man is already governed by God, a table can be an act of service, not surrender. Every table needs to be discerned, but every table is not a stress or a warfare.

Not every table a man sets becomes a place of loss; sometimes, like Mamre, it is simple hospitality. Hospitality is a spiritual gift that is given by the Holy Spirit. By all means, if it is your gift, use it.

Be not forgetful to entertain strangers: for thereby some have entertained angels unawares. (Hebrews 13:2)

It is when we think ALL tables are simple hospitality that we turn off discernment and may end up walking into a spiritual mess. Abraham's table at Mamre did not govern him — it served what God had already initiated. Discernment is knowing the difference. The enemy, the manipulator, the liar, cheater, thief, the mafia boss(?) is counting on the table looking benign. It will make his job easier.

Exactly. **Nothing has changed.** Only the setting did. The principle is the same across Scripture, relationships, and culture: **When someone comes for provision but not for covenant, the table is already misaligned.**

Those who go on "dates" for the food are not discerning connection, character, or future — they are responding to **appetite**. And appetite, when ungoverned, always treats the host as a means rather than a person.

This pattern is ancient. When people come for the food and not the relationship, the table has already been reduced. Appetite will sit where covenant never intended to. Nothing has changed — people still follow tables, when they should be following authority. They are still only worried about today instead of preparing for eternity.

Well—people have always followed bread. Authority has always thinned the crowd. This isn't about dating etiquette. It's about how appetite reveals motive. Scripture already told us how that ends.

The anointing to set a Godly table or a table of covenant is imparted to a man by God. Every table isn't that-- many are counterfeits that may actually be stacked against you. It depends on the host. Who is hosting any table that you sit at? You'd better know and you'd better know them by their fruit, and I don't mean their *apples*.

LOSS OF HOSTING RIGHTS

Adam, the Curse, and the loss of table authority is seen in Genesis 1–2). Adam is given dominion over creation, stewardship of the garden, effortless provision, and *unmediated access* to sustenance. Adam does not forage. He does not struggle. He does not host from scarcity. Provision flows because alignment is intact. That is governance.

After the Fall of man, provision becomes contested. God says,

Cursed is the ground because of you...
by the sweat of your face you shall eat bread.
(Genesis 3).

This is not merely punishment, it is **reordered governance**. Adam is no longer governing creation effortlessly, setting tables from abundance. Instead, provision resists him. food requires toil. sustenance becomes conditional. The ground no longer cooperates.

The Fall did not only affect Adam's labor, it affected his capacity to host from abundance. In other words, scarcity replaces overflow, effort replaces ease, survival replaces stewardship. A man struggling to feed himself cannot easily set covenant tables for others, not because God forbids it but because governance has been fractured.

This explains several Biblical patterns. Hospitality later requires intentional righteousness (Abraham). Covenant tables are rare and sacred. Why ungodly tables often operate through control and extraction. Why famine, drought, and scarcity become spiritual themes. Why Jesus restoring provision (feeding multitudes) is messianic. Jesus doesn't just feed people. He restores table authority.

Hosting now requires labor, discernment, and righteousness; it is not simply done by default authority.

The devil took the Fall as an opportunity to begin to use food, since it was harder to come by, as a temptation. We see that in both the Old Testament and in the New Testament.

Remember, they followed Jesus for food. But at least He was a Godly table whether they accepted Him or not. What Jesus offered was clean without ulterior motives.

People followed Jesus for provision. The Gospels are explicit about this. After the feeding miracles, Jesus says plainly, "You seek Me, not because you saw the signs, but because you ate the loaves and were filled." (John 6:26)

Many were drawn by food, healing, relief, miracles. Not all by discipleship or submission to His authority. That's why, when Jesus shifts from bread to identify Himself as Bread, many leave. Appetite brought them; authority sent them away.

Paul addresses this directly in 1 Corinthians 11. The issue wasn't hunger itself, it was misunderstanding the table. Some believers were treating Communion like a common meal and rushing ahead to eat. They were getting drunk, ignoring the poor, turning a covenant table into a satisfaction table. So, Paul says, in essence, If you are hungry, eat at home first. Don't bring ungoverned appetite to a covenant table.

Why?

Because Communion is not about filling the stomach, relieving hunger, or equalizing discomfort. Paul didn't say this, but I will: *It is not about seeing what you can get for free while coming to watch the show of miracles.*

It is about discerning the Lord's body, recognizing authority, entering and honoring covenant, understanding what the table represents

When appetite governs the table, people miss the meaning of the covenant. Crowds left Jesus when bread stopped. Wonder if there will be crowds when free donuts and coffee are no longer in the lobby? Appetite was what kept Israel stayed in the wilderness. Corinth corrupted Communion. Appetite is what keeps delaying authority.

How many of you have seen the little TikTok where a toddler is given a snack and told not to eat it until their parent returns from the kitchen or wherever? Immediate gratification is what delays authority. If God can't trust you with food, what else can he not trust you with?

Do you want flesh or soul gratification or authority in the Kingdom?

People followed Jesus for bread, but not all were willing to submit to His authority. Paul had to tell them, if you're hungry, eat at home. Because hunger has a way of drowning out discernment and food has a way of drowning out the voice of God to him who should be hearing it.

Appetite tests authority long before authority is entrusted.

After the Fall, food was no longer governed; it was contested. With that contest came the loss of effortless authority to host. When Adam fell, provision resisted him. A man struggling to eat cannot easily become a host of any kind and least of all a host of covenant for others. In Eden the table was effortless. After the Fall, provision was contested.

Jezebel used food to manipulate.

Melchizedek brought righteous provision and was authorized as a priest over the table.

Jesus restored provision

> But they shall sit every man under his vine and under his fig tree; and none shall make them afraid: for the mouth of the LORD of hosts hath spoken it.
> (Micah 4:4)

This verse describes the opposite of a hostile table. It shows authority intact. appetite governed. provision secured. peace established. In other words, When authority is settled, tables become safe.

Well—when a man is under his own vine, he doesn't eat in fear, and he doesn't host with hidden terms. Scripture's picture of Peace is not a crowded table, but a man secure enough to sit under his own vine and invite others without false motives and without fear.

FALSE TABLES- COUNTERFEIT HOSTS

If a person has lost hosting authority or table setting 'grace', in that vacuum an enemy type tries to swoop in and impersonate or tries to assume power? *False Tables. Counterfeit Hosts.* When hosting authority is vacated, something always tries to fill the space. Scripture consistently shows this pattern. Authority is never left neutral. When God-given governance is abdicated, something else moves to occupy the role. This is not because God loses control it's because governance on earth is stewarded, not automatic.

Hosting Authority is a real spiritual function. To "host" biblically is not just to provide food. It is to set atmosphere, define terms, determine what is permitted, establish boundaries, and influence allegiance. That's why tables are so spiritually charged. When a person loses discernment. righteous authority, covenant alignment, or self-governance, they don't just lose *capacity* — they create a **vacuum**. And vacuums invite substitutes.

Do counterfeit hosts move in? Yes —
repeatedly. Not randomly. Strategically. The enemy
does not usually attack head-on. He impersonates
function. He doesn't invent tables. He copies them.
That's why counterfeit hosts often look generous,
powerful, resourced, confident, well-positioned, But
their provision always comes with unspoken terms.

This is exactly what happened in Scripture. When
Adam's authority fractured, the ground resisted him,
then scarcity became leverage. When true prophets
fled, Jezebel hosted false ones. When priesthood
corrupted, political power crept into sacred space.
When discernment failed, appetite took over. When
governance weakened, patronage replaced covenant.
False tables don't appear where authority is intact,
they appear where authority has been surrendered,
exhausted, or confused.

Counterfeit hosts share telltale traits. They offer
provision without covenant. They demand loyalty
without righteousness. They expect silence in
exchange for sustenance. They confuse generosity
with control. They resent independence. They punish
discernment. They punish thinking. They are the *do as
I say* and *because I said so crowd*. They may feed you,
but they also believe they own you. They believe that
feeding you is for the purpose of owning. That's how
you know the table is false.

This answers a question many people feel but can't articulate *"Why did things get worse when I lost my footing?* Because loss of hosting authority doesn't leave a neutral gap. It creates an opportunity for impersonation.

This does not mean every struggle invites demons, or that every meal is spiritual warfare, or that every host is suspect. It does mean that authority must be actively stewarded — or it will be passively replaced.

False tables thrive where true hosting authority has been surrendered. When covenant hosting weakens, counterfeit hosts move in to impersonate provision. The enemy does not create tables; he steals to occupy vacated ones. If that means he has to trick you out of authority, that is what he will do. If that means he will begin a slow seduction to get you to give up authority, then he will try that. Loss of governance invites imitation, not absence.

Counterfeit hosts do not overthrow authority, they replace what has already been laid down.

WHEN PRESENCE BECOMES PARTICIPATION

Where you place yourself speaks before you do. Your feet often consent before your mouth does. You don't end up somewhere by accident for long.

One of the most misunderstood realities of authority is that presence is rarely neutral. In many settings, relational, spiritual, institutional, or transactional showing up is interpreted as agreement, even when no words are spoken. Authority systems read proximity as consent.

Most people believe the being somewhere is inherently benign. They think saying things like, *I was just there. I didn't say anything. I didn't agree. Or, I was only observing*, lets them out of responsibility.

In Bible days getting somewhere was a big deal. One did not find himself accidentally somewhere. It took quite an effort to get from one town to another or from one city to another.

Authority does not wait for verbal contracts. It watches to see who stays, who leaves, who remains silent, who speaks, who keeps returning to a given place. From this information, it draws conclusions.

The Biblical pattern is that silence and presence carry weight. Scripture repeatedly shows that being present authorizes atmospheres. silence can be read as alignment. lingering implies tolerance. repeated attendance signals acceptance. This is why Jesus *leaves* certain spaces, prophets *refuse* certain tables, apostles *withdraw* from corrupt fellowship. They understand something crucial. You cannot sit in a place indefinitely and remain uninvolved. This Becomes Dangerous. Presence becomes participation when boundaries are assumed instead of stated, silence is interpreted as approval. Attendance replaces discernment. This is how people become associated with things they never endorsed. are held accountable for decisions they never made. lose authority without realizing it. Not through rebellion but through unexamined proximity.

Presence does not remain passive for long. If authority is operating in a space, presence will eventually be interpreted as participation. If you stay seated long enough, the table will assume your consent.

When you start asking, *How did I end up here? I never agreed to this. Why am I responsible?* And start asking the right question, *"Why did I stay* The right question restores authority.

Because once people can *see* tables, they must learn when presence itself becomes a vote. Once people can see tables, they must learn when presence itself becomes a vote. Your face can appear on a Zoom call simply because attendance was required. You may never say a word. The microphone stays muted. And yet—you were there. Sometimes you are responsible to know what happened in that meeting, because you were there.

Do you think you'd be responsible for being in a getaway car at a bank robbery? Criminal and corrupt tables can be very damaging to a reputation, a career, or even a life.

Dinah, the daughter of Jacob, in Book of Genesis 34, her presence became exposure. Scripture says something deceptively simple *"Dinah… went out to see the daughters of the land."* This was not brunch, but it was unstructured exposure. Dinah was the daughter of a patriarch. She was sister to powerful sons (by this time, many of the twelve). She was part of a covenant family. She was not unprotected by status, and yet, she went out alone.

That detail is not incidental. Scripture includes it because it explains how the table turned. Dinah made a critical discernment error. Dinah did not go out to sin. She didn't go out to meet a man or go on a sneak date.

I used to be a server in a restaurant and that's when I realized that a lot of men who enter those places think that just because you're there, or even because you work there that you are there for their convenience or their conversation. I'm there to work, but it could be that the *kind* of place where I worked carried a weight that I hadn't realized. It wasn't a sleaze bar, but neither was it a family style restaurant.

Presence without protection is interpreted as availability. She entered a space not governed by her family's authority and not aligned with covenant culture. It was also not overseen by those who could intervene.

She *showed up* — and the system she entered assigned meaning to her presence. That table Turned on Dinah. What began as perhaps an observation outing, or a hike became exposure, violation, negotiation, and political manipulation.

After the assault, the situation escalates into bargaining, forced alliance, covenant language used falsely, and it became about violence and retaliation.

This is exactly what happens when a table turns hostile. Initial presence is misread. People attempt to blame the victim—he shouldn't have been there. Or, she was asking for it. Authority is bypassed.

Terms are imposed after the fact. Dinah never consented — but the environment did not care—she was there.

Discernment failures upstream create vulnerability downstream. Know where your presence will be interpreted — and by whom."

Know when not to go, and when not to go alone. Know how presence becomes participation in hostile systems. Know how covenant identity does not negate situational risk. Know that protection is not paranoia. Where you place yourself speaks before you do.

Dinah did not go out to give consent — but the place she entered was not governed by covenant, and it interpreted her presence for her. Not every table turns hostile immediately — some wait until you are seated alone.

Presence is a form of permission. Attendance is often read as alignment. Silence does not stop authority from assigning meaning. You can disagree internally and still authorize externally.

HOSTILE TAKEOVERS

Not all *takeovers* announce themselves as hostile; some are friendly. Some arrive smiling. Some arrive to the table as helpful. Some arrive generous. Some arrive *"just trying to bless you.* So yes, there are hostile takeovers, and there are friendly takeovers.

Both seek the same thing: Control of atmosphere, access, and allegiance. The difference is tone, not intent.

Friendly, takeovers are more dangerous.

A hostile takeover triggers resistance. A friendly one invites consent. That's why Scripture warns us about deceptive bread, flattering words, smooth speech, and gifts with expectation. Friendly takeovers succeed because they feel safe. They don't seize authority. They assume it. This is where the gift of hospitality matters. Yes — the gift of hospitality is from God. Godly hospitality does not seek leverage, does not expect allegiance. It does not punish boundaries. does not manipulate proximity, does not resent independence. It feeds without owning.

Scripture lists hospitality as a spiritual grace, not a personality trait (Romans 12).

But even spiritual gifts can be abused and misused. Counterfeit hospitality always reveals itself over time. It becomes offended by discernment, resents delayed trust, grows impatient with boundaries, subtly shifts from giving to expecting. True hospitality remains free, even when refused. That's the test.

The governing distinction is that *Hospitality given by God nourishes without binding. Counterfeit hospitality feeds in order to govern.* Or even more simply: If provision requires allegiance, it is not hospitality.

Godly hospitality leaves you freer than it found you. Be sure to evaluate every invitation, all generosity, mentorship, relationship, and even dates. Nothing can be faked.

FALSE COMMUNION TABLE

A false communion table may be the most uncommon table of all. A false communion table is uncommon — but it is among the most serious when it occurs. A false communion table is rare because Communion is already sacred Most people who misuse power prefer *less obvious* tables (money, access, loyalty, silence).

It requires spiritual audacity To imitate covenant knowingly is not casual error; it is presumption. It carries accountability Scripture is clear that mishandling the Lord's Table places responsibility on the one who administers it, not the one who follows in good faith. Most counterfeit systems avoid it altogether; they don't need it.

When it *does* occur, it matters because Communion is a covenant table, not a symbol-only ritual. It involves representation of Christ's Body and Blood. It is meant to discern the Lord's Body, not improvise it. So the issue is not the color of wine, bread type, or setting.

The issue is reverence, authority, intent, alignment with Christ Himself. That's why Scripture says judgment concerns the administrators, not unsuspecting participants.

False communion is when the sacrament is administered without reverence, authority, or alignment. Unworthy administration (careless, misguided, or disordered leadership) False covenant (intentional imitation or mockery). You were a participant, not a host. If you followed perceived authority and did not intend to be deceived, responsibility does not transfer to the guest, and that's biblical. In Scripture, responsibility rests on the one who sets the table and administers covenant, not on the guest who discerns later.

False communion tables are rare, but they reveal the gravity of covenant. When they occur, Scripture places responsibility on those who administer the table — not those who followed in good faith. Covenant is not casual. And neither is its misuse.

You did not stumble into danger unknowingly and remain bound. You recognized, renounced, and realigned. That's how authority works.

If you've ever sat at a false or corrupt communion table, you will want to pray the following prayer: Before you pray, know this for your Peace. You are not guilty. You did not initiate. You did not design the table. You did not consecrate the elements. You followed perceived authority in good faith.

This prayer is order-based cleansing and realignment. This prayer deals with your conscience, your authority, your covering, and your peace.

A Prayer of Renunciation, Cleansing, and Table Reset

Father God,

In the Name of Jesus Christ, the true Son, the true sacrifice, the true covenant.

I acknowledge You as the only Author of covenant, the only One who sets holy tables, and the only One who consecrates bread and wine unto life.

Lord, I confess that there was a time
when I sat at a table I did not set,
under authority I trusted,
and I participated without full knowledge or discernment.

I declare before heaven and earth:
I did not consent to any false covenant,
I did not agree to any mockery of Your sacrifice,

**and I did not offer my faith, body, or spirit
to anything outside of Christ.**

If any act, symbol, word, or substance
was presented under the appearance of holy
communion
but lacked Your consecration, Your reverence, or
Your order,

I now renounce it.

I renounce:

- any unauthorized table

- any imitation covenant

- any misrepresentation of the Blood of Jesus

- any spiritual agreement made through
  ignorance, pressure, or misplaced trust

**I withdraw my presence, my faith, and my
authority from that table now.**

Lord Jesus,
You alone are the Mediator of the New Covenant.
Your Blood was not symbolic.
Your Body was not casual.
Your Table is not improvised.

**I ask You now to cleanse my conscience fully,
as Hebrews declares,
from any defilement not of my choosing.**

Where I followed leadership that had drifted,
release me from responsibility that was never mine.

Where I honored improperly,
restore my discernment without condemnation.

Where confusion entered,
let truth settle gently and completely.

I now declare a Table Reset.

Jesus Christ, I re-seat myself at **Your** table alone.

Let Your Blood speak over me —
not accusation, but redemption.
Not fear, but peace.
Not confusion, but order.

Lord, I receive again the true covenant, the true
covering, and the true authority of Christ.

Any residue of false symbolism, any lingering
unease,
any spiritual question mark —

I place it under the finished work of the Cross.

Holy Spirit, seal this prayer.

Let peace find a resting place in me.
Let discernment remain awake, not anxious.
Let wisdom replace retrospection.
Let authority return quietly to its seat.

I do not carry shame. I do not carry fear.
I do not carry responsibility for another man's table.

I am covered. I am aligned. I am clean.

In the mighty, unmatched Name of Jesus Christ,
Amen.

If you feel release from having prayed this prayer then you do not need to repeat it. You do **not** need to "check" whether it worked. You do **not** need to revisit that table again in your mind. Authority has been restored. Peace has a place to land.

STABLE AT THE TABLE

We must remain stable at the table. We are looking for stability at the table, not fables. We seek what is stable at the table, not what is flattering. A stable table sustains; a fabled one distracts. Stability belongs at the table, not stories designed to persuade.

We are not drawn to fables at the table; we are anchored by what is stable and true. *Stable* implies tested, load bearing, trustworthy. *Fables* implies exaggeration, manipulation, spectacle, illusion, lies, stealing and traps.

When you sit to eat with a ruler, consider carefully
what is before you…
Do not desire his delicacies, for they are deceptive
food. (Proverbs 23:1–3)

When God resets the table, it is proof that the old arrangement has expired.

Some fast food. Some fast from noise, validation, access, appetite, applause, compromise, explanation, and urgency. Those fasts reorder tables for stability faster than hunger ever could.

Some tables end because they failed. Others end because God has decided to feed you differently.

What happens after reset" is an *actual biblical pattern*. First you may feel like you have nothing because reset is not dramatic. But it is stabilization, reorientation, and re-governance. Reset marks your authority returning to its rightful place. Scripture rarely sensationalizes the aftermath. It records order being restored.

What happens when resent happens? What happens when authority returns?

1. **Noise Decreases**. After a divine reset, confusion fades, urgency lessens, emotional pressure lifts but because governance has returned. Reset restores *order before outcome*.

2. **Appetite Loses Its Voice**. Hunger doesn't disappear, but it no longer decides, it no longer dictates; it is no longer running the show. People notice fewer impulsive decisions, less desperation, clearer "no's". There are fewer delayed gratification moments, but they are without anxiety. That's authority re-seated.

3. **False Tables Lose Access.** After reset invitations stop coming. Manipulative hosts retreat. Counterfeit opportunities dry up, not because you're hiding, but because your agreement is gone.

Tables only work where consent exists.

4. **Identity Stabilizes**, whereas before, these questions may have persisted, *Who am I?* But after reset, I know who I am. We stop auditioning and over-explaining. We stop over-performing. We stop negotiating our worth. Authority no longer needs proving.

5. **Provision Re-aligns**. Provision often returns slower, cleaner, less flashy, more sustainable. Confusion can result here. God doesn't rush to *replace* what was lost. He replaces how it was being governed.

6. **Discernment Sharpens** after reset. From now on, red flags register earlier. Discomfort is heeded. Peace becomes a guide again. People who have been through this process tend to say, *"I don't know how I know, but I just know."* That's not intuition. That's authority, finally settled inside.

7. **Peace Finds a Place to Land**. After reset, Peace stays. Rest becomes possible. Vigilance relaxes. The test dove doesn't keep flying, it finds a landing and resting place. Reset answers the question *Is there a place for Peace to rest again?*

Reset is not loss, punishment, or emptiness; it is recovery of governance. It is the return of clarity, and the re-seating of authority. Reset is not the end of something. It is the restoration of order. Reset doesn't feel dramatic, it feels quiet; and that's how you know it worked.

Give God the Glory, and **Amen.**

I seal this message, these decrees and declarations and prayers across every realm, age, era, dimension, and timeline, past present and future and to infinity. I seal them with the Blood of Jesus and the Holy Spirit of Promise.

Let every retaliation against this word, these prayers, these decrees and declarations spoken, prayed, or said by the speaker, or heard by the listener, or anyone praying these words backfire without Mercy, to infinity against the evil perpetrator, in the Name of Jesus. Amen.

AMEN.

Dear Reader

Thank you for acquiring and reading this book, **<u>When The Table Is Set Against You.</u>**

Shalom,

Dr. Marlene Miles

Prayerbooks by this author

There are some books that are only prayers. You just open up the book and pray.

Prayers Against Barrenness: *For Success in Business and Life*

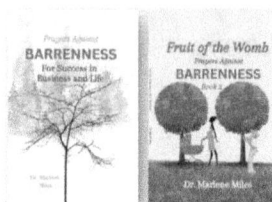

Fruit of the Womb: *Prayers Against Barrenness*

Beauty Curses, *Warfare Prayers Against*
https://a.co/d/5Xlc20M

Courts of Marriage: Prayers for Marriage in the Courts of Heaven *(prayerbook)* https://a.co/d/cNAdgAq

Courtroom Warfare @ Midnight *(prayerbook)*
https://a.co/d/5fc7Qdp

Demonic Cobwebs *(prayerbook)* https://a.co/d/fp9Oa2H

Every Evil Bird https://a.co/d/hF1kh1O

Gates of Thanksgiving

Spirits of Death, Hell & the Grave, Pass Over Me and My House

Throne of Grace: Courtroom Prayer

Warfare Prayer Against Poverty
https://a.co/d/bZ61lYu

Prayer Books by this Author

Prayer Manuals

FAKE FRIENDS: *Prayers Against Betrayers*

HOLIDAY WARFARE Prayer Manual (humorous) Surviving Family Gatherings All Year Long (without catching a case)

SOUL TIE Prayer Manual (The) Part of a 3-part series including a workbook.

MAD at DADDY Prayer Manual – part of a 3-part series including a workbook.

Healing the Sibling & Relative Wound Prayer Manual

Healing the Father-Son Wound Prayer Manual

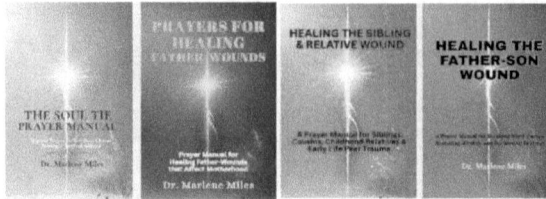

Prayers Against Barrenness: *For Success in Business and Life*

Breaking Curses of the Mother Prayer Manual

Other books by this author

Abundance of Jesus (The)
https://a.co/d/5gHJVed

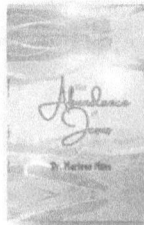

AK: The Adventures of the Agape Kid

Already Married in the Spirit: *Why You May Not Be Married in the Natural*

AMONG SOME THIEVES https://a.co/d/dkYT4ZV

Ancestral Powers

Anti-Marriage, *The Spirit of*

Backstabbers https://a.co/d/gi8iBxf

Barrenness, *Prayers Against* https://a.co/d/feUltIs

Battlefield of Marriage, *The*

Beware of the Dog: Prayers Against Dogs in the Dream.

Bless Your Food: *Let the Dining Table be Undefiled* *https://a.co/d/6oPMRDv*

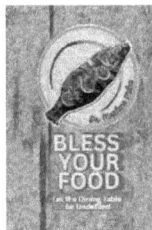

Blindsided: *Has the Old Man Bewitched You?* https://a.co/d/5O2fLLR

Break Free from Collective Captivity

Broken Spirits & Dry Bones

By Means of a Whorish Father

Caged Life: Get Out Alive!
https://a.co/d/bwPbksX

Casting Down Imaginations

Christ of God (The) 3-book series

Christ of God, Box Set, includes all three books

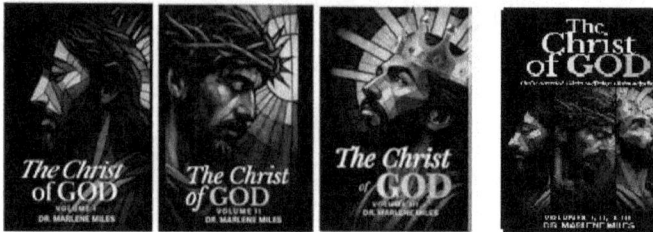

Churchzilla, The Wanna-Be, Supposed-to-be
Bride of Christ https://a.co/d/eAf5j3x

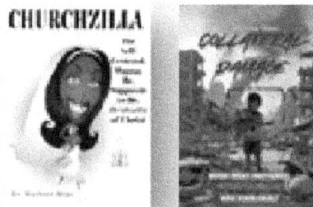

Collateral Damage: *When What Happened Spiritually Was Your Fault*

Demonic Cobwebs (prayerbook)

Demonic Time Bombs

Demons Hate Questions

Devil Loves Trauma, *The*

Devil Weapons: Unforgiveness, Bitterness,...

The Devourers: Thieves of Darkness 2

Do Not Swear by the Moon

Don't Refuse Me, Lord (4 book series)
https://a.co/d/idP34LG

Dream Defilement

The Emptiers: *Thieves of Darkness, 1*
https://a.co/d/5I4n5mc

Evil Touch

Failed Assignment

Fantasy Spirit Spouse https://a.co/d/hW7oYbX

FAT Demons (The): *Breaking Demonic Curses*
https://a.co/d/4kP8wV1

The Fold (5-book series)

- The Fold (Book 1)
- Name Your Seed (Book 2)
- The Poor Attitudes of Money (3)
- Do Not Orphan Your Seed (4)
- For the Sake of the Gospel (5)
- My Sowing Journal

Gang Ups: Touch Not God's Anointed

Gathered: No Longer Scattered
https://a.co/d/1i5DPIX

Getting Rid of Evil Spiritual Food

https://a.co/d/i2L3WYQ

got HEALING? Verses for Life

got LOVE? Verses for Life
https://a.co/d/8seXHPd

got HOPE? Verses for Life

got money? https://a.co/d/g2av41N

Has My Soul Been Sold? https://a.co/d/dyB8hhA

Here Come the Horns: *Skilled to Destroy*
https://a.co/d/cZiNnkP

Hidden Sins: Hidden Iniquity

https://a.co/d/4Mth0wa

How to Dental Assist

How to Dental Assist2: Be Productive, Not Wasteful

How to STOP Being a Blind Witch or Warlock

I Take It Back

Irresistible: Jesus' Triumphal Entry
https://a.co/d/dO9IfEC

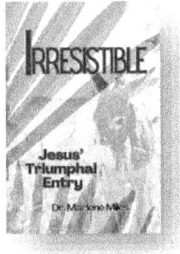

Legacy

Let Me Have A Dollar's Worth
https://a.co/d/h8F8XgE

Level the Playing Field

Living for the NOW of God

Lose My Location https://a.co/d/crD6mV9

Love Breaks Your Heart

Mad At Daddy: Healing Father-Wounds that Affect Motherhood (book, workbook & prayer manual)

Made Perfect In Love

Mammon https://a.co/d/29yhMG7

Man Safari, *The*

Marriage Ed. Rules of Engagement & Marriage

Made Perfect in Love

Money Hunters: Beware of Those

Money on the Altar https://a.co/d/4EqJ2Nr

Mulberry Tree, *The* https://a.co/d/9nR9rRb

Motherboard (The) - *Soul Prosperity Series*

Name Your Seed

Occupy: *Until I Return* https://a.co/d/bZ7ztUy

Opponent, Adversary, or Enemy?: Fight The Right Battle with the Right Weapons

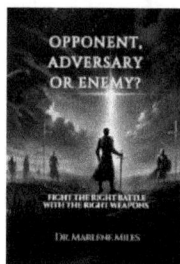

Plantation Souls

Players Gonna Play

Portals: Shut the Front Door: Prayers to Close Evil Portals.

Power Money: Nine Times the Tithe

https://a.co/d/gRt41gy

The Power to Get Wealth
https://a.co/d/e4ub4Ov

Powers Above

The Robe, Part 1, The Lessons of Joseph

The Robe, Part II, The Lessons of Joseph

Seasons of Grief

Seasons of Siege: GOD IS COMING

Seasons of Waiting

Seasons of War

Second Marriage, Third--, *Any Marriage*

https://a.co/d/6m6GN4N

Seducing Spirits: Idolatry & Whoredoms

https://a.co/d/4Jq4WEs

Shut the Front Door: *Prayers to Close Portals*
https://a.co/d/cH4TWJj

Sift You Like Wheat

Six Men Short: What Has Happened to all the Men?

SLAVE

Sleep Afflictions & Really Bad Dreams
https://a.co/d/f8sDmgv

Soul Prosperity soul prosperity series 3

https://a.co/d/5p8YvCN

Soul Ties: How Soul Ties Form, and How To Break Them (book, workbook & prayer manual)

Souls Captivity soul prosperity series 2

The Spirit of Anti-Marriage

The Spirit of Poverty https://a.co/d/abV2o2e

Spiritual Thieves https://a.co/d/eqPPz33

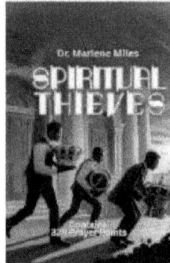

StarStruck- Triangular Power series.

SUNBLOCK- Triangular Power series.

The Swallowers: *Thieves of Darkness*, 3

Take It Back

This Is NOT That: How to Keep Demons from Coming at You

Time Is of the Essence

Too Many Wives: *Why You Have Lady Problems*

Tormenting Spirits   https://a.co/d/dAogEJf

Toxic Souls

Triangular Power *(series),* Powers Above, SUNBLOCK, Do Not Swear by the Moon, STARSTRUCK

Unbreak My Heart: *Don't Let Me Die*

Uncontested Doom

Unguarded Hours, *The*

Unseen Life, *The* (forthcoming)

Upgrade: How to Get Out of Survival Mode Toxic Souls (Book 2 of series) , Legacy (Book 3 of series)

The Wasters: *Thieves of Darkness,* Bk 2
https://a.co/d/bUvI9Jo

What Have You to Declare? What Do You Have With You from Where You've Been?

When I Was A Child, *I Prayed As a Child*

When the Devourer is Rebuked

https://a.co/d/1HVv8oq

When the Table Is set Against You

WTH? Get Me Out of This Hell
https://a.co/d/a7WBGJh

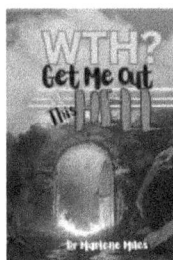

The Wilderness Romance *(series)* This series is about conducting a Godly relationship and marriage with someone who is a Wilderness person. It is about how to recognize it and navigate through it. These books are about how not to get caught up in such.

- *The Social Wilderness*
- *The Sexual Wilderness*
- *The Spiritual Wilderness*

Other Series

The Fold (a series on Godly finances) https://a.co/d/4hz3unj

Soul Prosperity Series https://a.co/d/bz2M42q

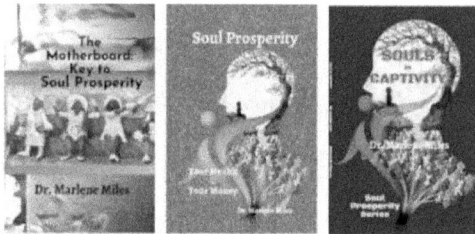

Spirit Spouse books

https://a.co/d/9VehDSo

https://a.co/d/97sKOwm

Battlefield of Marriage, The

https://a.co/d/eUDzizO

Players Gonna Play

https://a.co/d/2hzGw3N

Sent Spirit Spouse (can someone send you a spirit spouse? This book is not yet released.)

Matters of the Heart, Made Perfect in Love
https://a.co/d/70MQW3O , Love Breaks Your Heart https://a.co/d/4KvuQLZ, Unbreak My Heart https://a.co/d/84ceZ6M Broken Spirits & Dry Bones https://a.co/d/e6iedNP

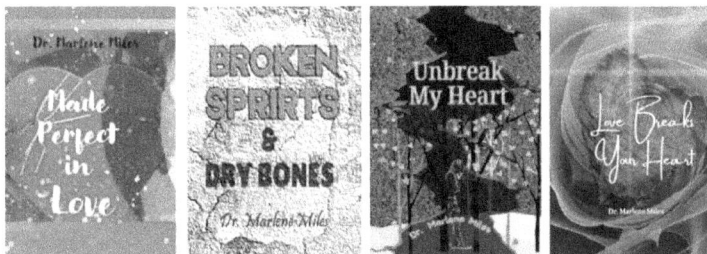

Thieves of Darkness series

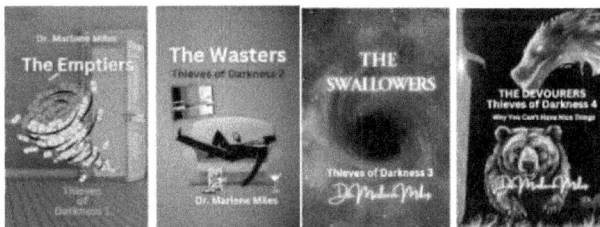

The Emptiers https://a.co/d/heio0dO

The Wasters https://a.co/d/5TG1iNQ

The Swallowers https://a.co/d/1jWhM6G

The Devourers: Why We Can't Have Nice Things https://a.co/d/87Tejbf

Spiritual Thieves

Triangular Powers https://a.co/d/aUCjAWC

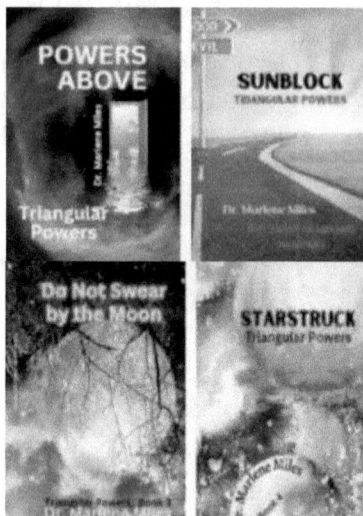

Upgrade (series) *How to Get Out of Survival Mode*
https://a.co/d/aTERhX0

We Get Along, Right? Compatibility for Couples –
(book & workbook)

www.ingramcontent.com/pod-product-compliance
Lightning Source LLC
LaVergne TN
LVHW052028080426
835513LV00018B/2229